Theological Construction— or Destruction?

An Analysis of the Theology of Bishop K. H. Ting (Ding Guangxun)

Theological Construction— or Destruction?

An Analysis of the Theology of Bishop K. H. Ting (Ding Guangxun)

Li Xinyuan

Editor's Note: Over the past year, the publication of *The Collected Essays of Bishop Ding* (*Ding Guangxun Wen Ji*) has become controversial topic among Chinese Christians. Li Xinyuan's critique was originally published in Chinese in the *Christian Life Quarterly* to alert readers to the potential danger that Ding's theology creates for the Chinese Church. Li's analysis places Ding's "theological thought" under the clear light of the Word of God.

Christian Life Press, Inc.
Streamwood, Illinois

Great Commission Center International
Mountain View, California

Theological Construction—or Destruction? An Analysis of the Theology of Bishop K. H. Ting (Ding Guangxun) by Li Xinyuan

© 2003 by Christian Life Press, Inc.

Christian Life Press, Inc.
670 Bonded Parkway, Streamwood, Illinois 60107
Phone: 630.837.7551 • Fax: 630.837.7552
E-mail: cclife@cclife.org • Website: www.cclife.org

Great Commission Center International
1101 San Antonio Road, Suite 400, Mountain View, California 94043
Phone: 650.968.2985 • Fax: 650.968.4856
E-mail: info@gcciusa.org • Website: www.gcciusa.org

First Published 2004

Printed in Hong Kong
Cover design and layout by Dona Diehl

ISBN: 0-9719016-1-9

Table of Contents

Foreword

Spiritual warfare intensifies as end time draws near. It is clear from the beginning that ultimately, every person on earth has to face the final all-important question: belief or unbelief. Churches today, without exception, are meeting this challenge headon!

Overseas Chinese churches have to confront the inroads of cults, the lingering effect of the old modernist theology, and the pervasive influence of postmodernism (the denial of absolute truth, the death of God and self-deification). Churches in Mainland China however, in addition to all the above snares of perdition, has to endure an incessant pressure from the so-called "Theological Construction" campaign.

This campaign has been initiated and aggressively promoted in the past few years by Bishop K.H. Ting (Ding Guangxun) the leading spokesman of the Three-Self Patriotic Movement. His central theme is the replacement of the doctrine of justification by faith with a new doctrine of justification by love (i.e. salvation by good works). His argument: God is love, those who have love belong to God and will go to heaven regardless of whether they believe in Christ or not. Such teaching is as unbiblical as it is dangerous. Since it enjoys the support of the official Three-Self church and its seminaries, its potential damage to Christians in China cannot be overstated.

It pains us to think that the church in China, which was built through the lives, labor and martyrdoms of countless missionaries and national workers over the past two centuries, may now be led astray by one man's theological adventure—a concoction of Wu Yaozong, Karl Marx, Whitehead and de Chardin combined with Ting's own speculations! A candid biblical response is therefore necessary.

We are happy for the publication of the English version of *Theological Consturction—Or Destruction?—An Analysis of the Theology of Bishop K. H. Ting (Ding Guangxun)* originally writtern in Chinese by brother Li Xinyuan, a Bible scholar and apologist. The book provides a succinct exposition as well as a Bible-based refutation of Ting's Theological Construction and its implications. This is a book that should be read by all who are concerned for the church in China.

Our heart-felt appreciation goes to Brother John Tai and Rev. Barnabas Cheung for the translation work; and to Brother Paul Hoffman, Dr. Chi-Yu King and Dr. Samuel C. Y. Ling for the proofreading, and to brother Tony Lambert, veteran China researcher for his introductory article "The Career and Theology of Bishop K. H. Ting."

May this volume be instrumental in God's hand to bring spiritual discernment, vigilance and renewal to churches both in China and worldwide.

Thomas Wang
October, 2003

Preface

The goal in publishing the compilation of analyses that make up "An Example of the 'Unbelieving Faction'" is to provide a readers' reference for understanding the anti-biblical nature of the Ding Guangxun *Wen Ji* (*Ding Guangxun Collection of Works*).

In an article in *Tianfeng*, October, 2001 published after the publication of *Wen Ji*, Mr. Ding Guangxun began a less thinly veiled and more thorough effort to eradicate the concept of justification by faith. This fact deserves serious attention of any Chinese Christian who is willing to hold fast to the truths of the Bible. Ding believes that there are only two books in the Bible—Romans and Galatians—that speak of justification by faith, and that "the Bible has also recorded those who disagree with justification by faith, most typically in the book of James.... The book of James at a minimum questioned the concept of justification by faith" (*Tianfeng*, October 2001).

To achieve his goal of eradicating the concept of justification by faith, Mr. Ding Guangxun was willing to create contradictions, allowing one section of the Bible to question another section of the Holy Book. The internal coherence of the revelation of the Holy Spirit and the absolute wholeness of the framework of God's words once again received Mr. Ding's contempt and trampling.

Justification by faith is the bedrock of the Christian faith. However, in the eyes of Mr. Ding Guangxun, the eradication of justification by faith is necessary to remove the distinction between believers and non-believers, thereby making Christianity "a Christian faith that will bring important messages to the world." This rhetoric offers much in helping us to understand the nature of the belief system of today's unbelieving faction.

Before he died, the Apostle Paul said to Timothy: "I have fought the good fight, I have finished the race, I have kept the faith. Now there is in store for me the crown of righteousness, which the Lord, the righteous Judge, will award to me on that day—and not only to me, but also to all who have longed for his appearing" (2 Timothy 4: 7-8).

This passage has encouraged many to remain faithful to Christ's truths to the end of their earthly lives. However, its citation here is also a reflection of our grief for Mr. Ding Guangxun, because everything he says today is in direct opposition to what Paul said at a similar period in his life. In the past 50 years, Mr. Ding has fought many fights and run many races. However, those fights were not the fights of those Christians who uphold the truth, and those races were in direct opposition to the fundamental truths. What will a just and righteous God reserve for someone who has fought such fights and run such races?

We hope that Mr. Ding Guangxun and his colleagues can repent before the God who judges righteously, thereby receiving salvation through faith!

Let us pray for him and his followers.

Li Xingyuan
February 6, 2003

Introduction

The Career and Theology
of Bishop K. H. Ting

Tony Lambert

The last few years have seen the promotion by Bishop Ding Guangxun (K. H. Ting), former head of both the China Christian Council (CCC) and the Three Self Patriotic Movement (TSPM), of a campaign for theological construction which is compatible with socialism. Pastors and seminary students in many places across China have been encouraged to attend meetings to study Ding's *Essays*, which were first published in 1998. Ding has strongly attacked evangelicals, whom he admits are the overwhelming majority in the Chinese Protestant church. In the preface to a book published in September 2000 he has also attacked the centrality of justification by faith, the reliability and inerrancy of the Bible and the necessity for faith in Christ, downplaying the difference between faith and unbelief.[1]

Nanjing Seminary, the most prestigious in the country, has been purged of evangelicals, first in 1999 when three students were dismissed ostensibly for refusing to sing Communist Party anthems in the seminary chapel. Three prominent graduates then resigned in protest. In 2000 various members of the faculty were removed or sidelined. A promising young evangelical theological scholar was also dismissed.[2] This politicized campaign for theological construction can therefore not be dismissed as a gentlemanly theological debate. It has already seriously impacted people's lives. Ding's theology and actions have aroused strong opposition from evangelicals in China and throughout the world.

It is helpful, therefore, to understand the background to Bishop Ding's long career and his developing theology. Although retired from his posts as head of the TSPM and CCC, Bishop Ding clearly

retains a significant influence. He appears bent on making a perma-
nent mark on Chinese theology. The appearance of the *Essays*, therefore, seems an opportune time for some reflection on the Bishop's
theology and career from an evangelical perspective. Li Xinyuan
gives a detailed critique from the perspective of a Chinese Christian
deeply rooted in Scripture. My own article is devoted to an overview
of Bishop Ding's career concentrating on the period up to the end
of the Cultural Revolution. It is meant to provide an overview and
introduction for readers wishing to know some background history.

Bishop Ding was born on September 20, 1915 in Shanghai—
only four years after the overthrow of the Qing dynasty by Sun Yat-
sen. Already China was sliding into the chaos and misery of the War-
lord era. Ding's father was a banker; his father and mother were both
Christians. Ding's maternal grandfather had been an Anglican minister. The boy was sent to St. John's University in Shanghai, which was
run by the American Episcopal Church, to study engineering. He
later changed to theology at the urging of his mother who prayed
that her son, too, would become an Anglican minister.

During the thirties Ding first came into contact with Wu
Yaozong, who later became the first leader of the Three Self
movement. By his own account, Ding was greatly impressed by Wu's
radical theology which encouraged him to sideline his Greek text-
books and the evangelical "Thirty-Nine Articles" of the Church of England in favor of the "question of national salvation." Wu told him
that "only after the social system in China underwent a basic change
would objective conditions emerge to make personal transformation
possible." Thus, from his youth, Ding appears to have chosen a theology of political liberation in preference to the evangelical gospel
which stresses personal transformation through faith in Christ.

Wu was influential in the YMCA in Shanghai. Between 1938-
1943 Ding was active as Student Secretary of the Shanghai "Y." This
was during the difficult years of the Japanese occupation. Ding encouraged young Christians and non-Christians to meet together to
discuss social and political questions, and hold Bible studies. The
emphasis was on transforming the social system (*China & Ourselves*
May 1980). Young Christian intellectuals were indignant about the
fate of their country. The underground Communist Party made the
YMCA a particular target in its campaign to win the allegiance of Chi-

nese youth. Much of the post-1949 leadership of the TSPM has come from those who had been involved with the YMCAs or YWCAs (Wickerai, p. 125). In 1979 Ding related to a visiting Canadian, Dr. Gardner, his "conversion" experience from orthodox Christian faith to a political social gospel:

> There was one type of Christian belief which we felt to be irrelevant. We, or many of us gave it up. This type said that all the trouble in China was due to something wrong in the hearts of human beings; therefore the first thing that Christians wanted to do was to change people's hearts... We moved to a Christian faith which has something to say about the transformation of the social system. (Gardner 1979)

Quite clearly, as a young man Ding had jettisoned orthodox, evangelical Christianity and personal salvation.

In 1942 Ding was ordained as a priest in the "Sheng Gong Hui" (Anglican Church of China). In the same year he married Kuo Siu May from Wuhan who had studied at St. Mary's Hall, an Anglican high school in Shanghai and at Beijing (then Yenching) University. For the next three years he served as pastor of the International Church in Shanghai. However, in 1946 he moved to Canada to become the Missions Secretary of the Student Christian Movement. The SCM, which only much later was to be eclipsed worldwide by the evangelical InterVarsity Fellowship, was very liberal in its theology. After a year, they moved to New York where Ding completed a Master's Degree at Union Theological Seminary, then, as now, a bastion of "progressive" theology. In 1981, a profile on Ding published by Keston College, made the following interesting comment:

> In the late forties K H Ding was a leading figure on the SCM—a body at that time associated in China with "progressive" socialist theology, which had a distinct lack of respect for denominational ties. It is not surprising that he regarded the advent of the Communists as a blessing for the Chinese people.

In 1948, Ding, still only 33, moved yet again, this time to Geneva, Switzerland, to work as Secretary of the World Student Christian Federation. In China the savage civil war between Communists and Nationalists was fast reaching a decisive conclusion. Ding went to Prague in May 1949 to attend the Stalinist-dominated World Peace

Council where he again met Wu Yaozong. Wu, Ding later said, talked to him at length about the role of the church in the new Communist society and the important place of the Communist Party's "United Front" policy. Wu also told him that there would have to be 'extensive and intensive education' about the new religious policy among all religious believers, the general public and Party cadres (Whitehead 1989, 155).

In 1950 the Korean War broke out. The Ding family was placed in difficulties concerning visas as Ding's wife and son were then living in the United States. But eventually they were able to stay on in Geneva for a further year. Despite the warnings of some Western friends, they flew to Hong Kong and arrived back in Shanghai in late August 1951. Ding returned to China willingly as an important young Christian leader ready to do his part under the new Communist government.

In February 1952 Ding published his first theological article in *Tianfeng*, the mouthpiece of the TSPM. In this he blatantly drew a political meaning from God's question to Adam in the Garden of Even after the Fall ("Adam, where are you?" Genesis 3:6-13). According to Ding this was a call for political participation by Chinese Christians in the Communist Party's mass political campaigns, which caused such immense suffering in the 1950s and 1960s:

> Today we are surrounded on all sides by the high tide of the [Party's] 'Three Antis Campaign.' If we Christians confess and repent before God and before the People our own heavy burden will be cast aside. Then we can throw ourselves bravely into this movement of the entire People. (*Tianfeng*, February, 1952)

Ding stated enthusiastically that the church had failed, but the Party had succeeded under the banner of Mao:

> In the era when darkness ruled [i.e. pre-1949] not a few Christians shone like "candles in a dark room." But today when "The east is red and the sun rises" [a clear reference to Chairman Mao taken from the popular Communist anthem] we have no cause for self-congratulation. In the radiance of the People's high morality our [Christian] "bright lamps" are lusterless. Faced with the manifestation of their high morals and their vast movement opposing every kind of crime we are like Adam, having no way of escaping God's searching question: "Where are you?"

A clearer statement that the gospel had failed and had been effectively replaced by Maoism can hardly be imagined. Ding also extolled revolutionary Marxist heroes:

> Today in farms, in factories and in armed resistance on the front-line [against the UN forces in Korea], ordinary people are producing extraordinary results every moment. Nourished by patriotism "they out of weakness were made strong and waxed valiant in fight" (Hebrews 11:34). They were those of whom the world was not worthy (v. 38). Inspired by the great spirit of the new democratic nation they have simply become a new kind of people in the world.

This extraordinary exegesis has clearly crossed the borderline between biblical Christianity and full-blooded Marxism. For Ding, rebirth by the Holy Spirit has been replaced by the Maoist "New Man." Although the rhetoric has been downplayed since, this train of thought in which Communist heroes set an example for the church is one which can be found in many of Ding's essays down to the present.

From the mid-1950s to the mid-1960s Ding often visited Wu Yaozong who had by then become the leading figure in the nascent TSPM. Ding was one of the youngest of a core of generally theologically-liberal church leaders who rallied to the Communist Party under Wu's leadership (Whitehead 1989, 10). The fifties were a tumultuous and agonizing time for the church. First, the missionaries were forced to leave. Then all financial support to the Chinese church from overseas was cut during the Korean War. Accusation campaigns tore the church apart. By the mid-1950s the denominational structures had largely been destroyed, to be replaced by the TSPM itself. Early on Ding showed his complete loyalty to the new government. In April 1952 he published a further article in *Tianfeng* comparing the death of Christ to the deaths of Communist revolutionary martyrs:

> Whether in German concentration camps, Turkish prisons, villages in old China or on Golgotha's cross "those of whom the world was not worthy ... all having obtained a good report through faith received not the promise..." The distant prospect which they viewed from afar by faith has become a reality which we can see with our eyes and touch with our hands in today's new world. Today those who have a new consciousness and new courage march forward in

the mainstream of history, causing all the forces of darkness to reel back in panic.

Previously he had made it plain he was not referring to Christians, but to a Czech Communist poet imprisoned by the Nazis, a Turkish political figure "imprisoned by reactionaries" and the Communist "White Haired Girl" (immortalized in Madame Mao's opera) who escaped from "the landlord's fiery hell." Here, the atoning work of Christ has been completely subsumed into the triumphant march of revolutionary Communism.

In June 1952 his name appeared eighth on a list of 140 signatures to a letter condemning the United States for supposedly using germ warfare in Korea. This was a mark of how high he had risen within a year of his return to China.

To facilitate the dismantling of the denominational structures, the TSPM held a meeting in Shanghai in August 1952 at which it was decided to close down eleven theological colleges and amalgamate them into the existing Nanjing Jinling Theological Seminary, one of the most liberal. The TSPM chose the Board of Directors and Ding was appointed the new principal. Thus began his long association with Jinling which has lasted (with a break during the Cultural Revolution) for over 45 years until the present day. After Western funds were cut off, financial support for the seminary came largely from rent of the property owned by the uniting schools, as well as church contributions. In the 1950s the students were expected to spend at least two days per week in political studies. In early 1953 Ding reportedly told them that full academic freedom prevailed but it was not "freedom to pervert the scriptures, spread rumors, oppose those fighting for right, or to uphold imperialism" (Bush 1970, 87-88).

In 1955, although still only aged 40, Ding was consecrated as a bishop of the Anglican Church for the diocese of Zhejiang near Shanghai. It should be noted that by that time the Anglican Church, as all other church denominations, was virtually defunct as an independent organization. The TSPM were well on the way to controlling all Protestant denominations. Ding's appointment at such a late stage is thought-provoking; it has certainly provided him with subversive influence and standing in ecumenical circles worldwide.

In 1955 Ding crossed swords with the redoubtable Wang Mingdao, leader of China's independent evangelicals. In a pamphlet,

We, Because of Faith, published in June of that year, Wang attacked the liberal theology of both Wu Yaozong and Ding, quoting their writings extensively to prove his point that there could be no compromise with a liberal theology which denied the basic tenets of the gospel. Wang openly criticized them as unbelievers for rejecting the Virgin Birth, the bodily resurrection of Christ and the full authority of the Scriptures (Mingdao 1996). A series of articles was then published in *Tianfeng* as part of an orchestrated national campaign to defame Wang Mingdao. In mid-August Ding published a long article attacking Wang in *Tianfeng* entitled "A Stern Warning to Wang Mingdao." One week earlier, on the night of August 7, Wang and his wife had already been arrested and disappeared into prison and labor-camp for a total of 23 years. However, the important issues raised by Wang Mingdao have not gone away: the graduates who resigned in 1999 from Nanjing seminary spoke approvingly of Wang's theology. Bishop Ding has expressed his irritation that the battles fought with Fundamentalists in the 1950s have to be fought all over again.

In 1956 a brief relaxation in repression occurred during the famous "Hundred Flowers" Campaign, when Mao at first encouraged people, especially intellectuals, to criticize the Party. Many Christians responded, complaining of discrimination, that children of believers were sometimes expelled from school, that atheistic propaganda was full of abuse against Christianity, etc. A provincial chairman of the TSPM even opposed the control of religious affairs by the government and said openly that the RAB was bureaucratic and had restricted religious affairs. The high-point of daring was perhaps reached by the famous evangelical leader Marcus Cheng who had joined the TSPM. In a speech widely publicized he quoted instances of churches being used as stables and a Party cadre calling on believers "to throw your God on the dung-heap." "Such blasphemy of God, to Christians is worse than reviling one's mother" (Bush 1970, 244-246). He was, with many others, to pay dearly for such forthrightness when Mao accused them of being counter-revolutionary rightists.

Ding delivered a lecture to his students in June 1957 just as the "Hundred Flowers" campaign was being phased out. He challenged the Communist stereotyped classification of all ideology and religion as either materialistic or idealistic, and attacked the Marxist view that Christianity is an opiate. Despite these forthright criticisms, Ding surprisingly emerged unscathed when Mao unleashed the "Anti-Rightist" campaign soon after (Jones 1962, 139). Most other Christians were not so fortunate: Marcus Cheng was purged from the TSPM and many others disappeared into labor camps. Between February 2 and May 13, 1958 a political studies conference was convened in Nanjing, attended by 240 local church workers and 96 seminary students. A number of Christians were condemned as rightists. The most prominent was Luther Shao, a leader of the Disciples. The pressure on him was so intense that he committed suicide by drowning in April 1959 (Bush 1970, 227).

During the mid-1950s, China was increasingly isolated from the outside world because of the American embargo. There were few foreign visitors and even fewer Chinese were allowed freely to travel overseas. However, Ding was one of a handful of privileged "patriotic" religious figures who went abroad to attend conferences and assure the outside world that China still enjoyed religious freedom. In the summer of 1956 he attended a preparatory meeting in London for the Anglican Lambeth Conference and also a meeting of the World Council of Churches in Hungary as an unofficial observer. Relations between China and the WCC were tense because of the Cold War. Ting told the WCC leaders in no uncertain terms that inviting former missionaries to speak about the situation of the church in China was viewed as continued imperialist involvement in the internal affairs of the Chinese church. For years after the WCC hesitated about uttering a word on the Chinese church.

In November 1957 he visited Hungary again—a year after the brutal Soviet suppression of the Hungarian uprising. He tells us what his thoughts were as the aircraft approached Budapest:

> We could not help but think of the dark days a year ago when the imperialists were carrying out their counter-revolutionary activities. When the workers' and farmers' revolutionary government was re-established, and Hungary with the help of Soviet Russia was able to suppress so quickly this counter-revolutionary revolt, our hearts were made peaceful again. Looking down from the air I could not help but think of Luke 15: "This your brother was dead and is alive; he was lost and is found; therefore let us make merry and be glad." (Jones, 1962, 127)

In 1961 Ting attended a Soviet-sponsored Peace Conference in

Prague and spoke at the Bethlehem Church there. This appears to be his last overseas visit for nearly twenty years until after the Cultural Revolution. Ding's willingness to be an official religious spokesperson calls to mind the similar role of church leaders in the Soviet Union and Eastern Europe who attended World Council of Churches' conferences in the days before the fall of the Berlin Wall.

1958 saw the unification of all the Protestant churches under the banner of the TSPM. The vast majority of churches were closed down leaving only a handful open in major cities. In Beijing the number was reduced from 64 to 4, in Shanghai from about 200 to 23. Pastors and church workers were thereby released for productive labor. Many people stopped attending the politicized remnant of churches and braver souls quietly met in their homes. On the eve of the Cultural Revolution the church in China was a ghost of its former self. By 1964 the number of full-time students at Nanjing Seminary had dwindled to only 25. There seemed little need to produce new pastors for a dying institution. In 1964 Ding said that a half-day each week was devoted to "political discussion" and that each student was required to give twenty days each year to productive work on the land. A little later he informed a visitor from Canada that no stigma was placed on anyone for his religious beliefs.

From the mid-1950s an ominous twilight had fallen across the church in China. Church membership, with some exceptions, dwindled. Many young people brought up in Christian families joined the Party. There seemed little future for the church. In 1966 the catastrophe of the Cultural Revolution erupted. The fanatical Red Guards, egged on by Mao, burnt Bibles and closed down the last few urban churches. Pastors and religious leaders were beaten, imprisoned and sent to labor-camps or to work in factories or in the countryside. China descended into a nightmare of political repression.

However, Bishop Ding escaped surprisingly unscathed from the Cultural Revolution. According to his own account, Nanjing Seminary was closed down and became the headquarters of the Red Guards in that city. He and the students spent some time helping the peasants plant vegetables and later they did translation work for a fertilizer factory and then translations of documents after China joined the United Nations in 1971 (*One World*, March 1988). Ding was given exceptionally preferential treatment. During the latter period of the Cultural Revolution, he was permitted to receive foreign visitors in Nanjing. He was allowed to speak to them as a quasi-government spokesman justifying Maoist policies which had obliterated the institutional church.

In an interview with E. H. Johnson in March 1973 Ting stated that the Red Guards in 1966 entered his home and church and took away books, the cross and the candlesticks but in a few months it was agreed that religion was to be respected and the books and religious objects were returned. He further told Johnson that ordained professional ministers and church-buildings were considered non-essential to Christian ministry. Both of course, had been ruthlessly banned since 1966 at the outbreak of the Cultural Revolution. Ding and his wife insisted that they and their sons as known Christians did not suffer any discrimination either at school or at work (Johnson 1973). If so, they must have been almost unique in China when reactionary family or class background doomed millions of people to suffer persecution from the left-wing extremists.

On October 22, 1976 Ding met with Eugene Stockwell at the Nanjing Seminary soon after the death of Mao and the downfall of the leftist "Gang of Four." Ding stated bluntly that "missionaries were tools of imperialist aggression." He also stated that: "with the new position and esteem of labor, many of our ministers wanted to identify themselves with the people around them in mental and manual labor. They feel they do not want to be full-time ministers." He also stressed how "there is a constant decrease in the number of Christians....With the imperialist background it is understandable that the number of believers would decline." Because of this "it is unthinkable to maintain a five-year [theological] course for students to educate them in an ivory tower to be a new elite. Christians will not support them anyway."

When asked by Stockwell whether he would agree that Christianity would die out in China Ding stated: "I would not be surprised if that would be the case." He denied the existence of concentration camps in China. His wife told Stockwell that "here [in China] we find every person is respected as a person... We love Chairman Mao for all he has taught us."[3]

In 1978 when the pragmatic Deng Xiaoping began to rise to

power and leftist Maoist influence was well on the wane, Ding met with Howard Hyman in Nanjing. He told Hyman that "Chinese Christians today are not eager to hold meetings in church buildings...The theological and liturgical concepts of building those churches was entirely Western." Ding doubted the effectiveness of Christian radio programs beamed into China from overseas. He also opposed the idea of evangelism to the vast Chinese population: "As far as I can see very few Chinese Christians today think that he or she has a call to evangelize China....It would not be fruitful to say the least for us to talk too much about evangelism, because we would be promoting a Western commodity" (*New China* magazine, Summer 1979). Ding's hostility to the Great Commission is clear.

In November 1979 Ding received Dr. John Gardner in Nanjing. He downplayed the suffering of Christians during the Cultural Revolution ("Religious people suffered, but there were other people who suffered more—the intellectuals...and old revolutionaries." He also made some astonishing comments excusing the Maoists:

> I should like to say something about those revolutionaries who tended to be very dogmatic and ultra-leftist. I do want to say something kind about them. I know they have done a lot of things that were bad in China and even cruel, but I like to think of them not as counter-revolutionaries or bad people.

When Gardner questioned whether one can really talk about the ultra-left having a sense of justice when one looks at the violence during the Cultural Revolution with its attacks on harmless, old intellectuals, Ding excused them in the following terms,

> When we look at a revolutionary situation then we have to be prepared to see all sorts of things happen. But these things are rather superficial. We have to look at the essence of a revolution. It was a bad thing for some of them to burn our Bibles but the very burning of the Bibles I think tells us how our Chinese people hate Western imperialism. (Gardner 1980)

Ding admitted to his visitors during the 1970s that small numbers of Christians in Nanjing were meeting in homes, but the above comments show clearly that as late as the late 1970s, he saw no real future for Christianity. His comments read strangely in view of the subsequent massive growth of the gospel over the past two decades and of the vast building program of churches (whose services are still very Western in style) and seminaries across China which he himself headed in the 1980s and 1990s. When Ding made his Maoist comments in the early- and mid-1970s there were no churches open in China at all. Today in 2003 there are about 50,000 legal Protestant churches and meeting-points! It is difficult to avoid the conclusion that his pronouncements were guided more by the prevailing political climate at the time than by a spiritual assessment of the situation. His theological views were clearly forged by a deep appreciation of Marxism and governed by the then-prevailing Maoism.

In 1978-79 the Communist Party decided to allow limited religious freedom which permitted churches and seminaries to re-open. Ding played a major role as the key Protestant church leader in China. He received many Christian delegations from overseas; he himself has been overseas on numerous occasions. For many years he played a prominent political role as one of the few religious members of the National People's Congress and the Chinese People's Political Consultative Committee. Throughout the eighties and into the nineties he acted as a church spokesman. His basic theological liberalism was changeable, depending on his audience. He could even sound Evangelical and Conservative compared to some of the extreme statements emanating from some radical members of the World Council of Churches. In 1989 Ding openly supported the student movement. He escaped public censure, but eventually retired from his post in the National People's Congress.

However, in November 1998 the TSPM and CCC held an important national conference in Jinan, Shandong. Here Ding unveiled his long-term, strategic plan for "theological construction" aimed at the total transformation of the Chinese church. Since then, what is in effect an old-style political campaign has gained momentum. Ding's statements have become more openly anti-evangelical. Many books and articles have poured from official church presses calling for diligent study of Ding's works. The aim is to re-educate theologians, seminary students and pastors in Ding's radical theology so that the entire Chinese church will be influenced at the grass-roots level. Those who dare to oppose this theological juggernaut are swept aside, losing their teaching posts or seminary places.

A battle for the soul of the Chinese church is thus underway. A clever smokescreen has been created to mislead Christians overseas. It is claimed theological construction is merely aimed at updating theology in accordance with the Bible and making it thoroughly indigenous and Chinese. Few would argue with Ding if this were the case. Indeed, Ding's most vociferous evangelical critics within the TSPM/CCC have called for Chinese Christians to engage seriously with the problems of modern society—not through a politicized theology, but by the thorough application of Biblical principles. These educated pastors and theologians within the CCC are warning Christians both in China and overseas that the "theological construction" campaign is aimed at the very heart of the gospel—attacking justification by faith, overturning the authority of Scripture and denying the unique centrality of Jesus Christ as the only way of salvation.

The massive revival and church growth in China of the last three decades is a work of God and a vindication of the biblical gospel. In the West, a pitiful liberalism has emptied churches and marginalized the influence of the gospel on society. It would be tragic if the Chinese church were to go down the same dead-end. Thankfully, many Chinese Christians are fully aware of the momentous issues at stake. By taking a stand, they suffer, for the gospel, centered on the Cross and Resurrection of Our Lord Jesus Christ. We in the West need to stand with them and learn from them as we seek revival and renewal of our own churches.

Notes

1. Zhongguo Jidujiao Shengjingguan Xueshu Yantao Hui Lunwenji (Essays from the Conference on Views of the Bible of the Chinese Christian Church), TSPM/CCC, Sept 2000, pp. 1-4.

2. The statements and letters of the students, graduates and Ji Tai have been widely circulated in Chinese on the Internet. See also *South China Morning Post* (Hong Kong), 28 June 1999.

3. Typed notes of interview with Dr. and Mrs. K. H. Ting by Eugene L. Stockwell, October 22, 1976, Nanjing.

(The bulk of this article was published in *China Insight*, March/April 2000.)

1

Faction of Unbelief

I wrote an analysis of Ding Guangxun's written works, entitled "An Example of 'Faction of Unbelief'"—see Appendix One of this book. Now, let me use the same title for an analysis of Ding's *Collected Essays* (hereafter simply called *Essays*), meaning collected articles, which has been hailed as a milestone of Chinese theology. First, we will provide a brief explanation of the term "faction of unbelief."

The term "faction of unbelief" first appeared in an article written by Wang Mingdao (the most famous Chinese evangelical leader of the twentieth century) in April 1929, entitled "How Long Will You Waver Between Two Opinions?" At that time Wang Mingdao stoutly defended the full authority and inspiration of the Bible against those leaders in the church, both Chinese and Western, who denied the basic doctrines of the Christian faith. The relevant section reads:

> The faction of unbelief has intentionally eliminated every important biblical principle, which is accepted by faith. Some of them publicly stated that these biblical principles are not acceptable. There were also others who said that we do not need to pay attention to these unimportant matters (in fact, these are extremely important). Still, there were those who changed what was clearly recorded in the Bible and provided erroneous interpretations.

> Although their statements might differ, they shared similar unbelief. They did not believe in God's omnipotence and omniscience. They did not believe the redemption, resurrection, and return of Christ. They were clearly unbelievers. Is it not appropriate to call them the faction of unbelief?

In the mid-1950s, Ding Guangxun, who by then was an up-and-coming leader in the Communist Party who supervised the Three Self Patriotic Movement which had taken over the church, raised this issue again. He said:

> What truly causes heartbreak is that today there are actually people who arbitrarily label others as the "faction of unbelief." What kind of behavior is this? We should be accountable to God for what we say. Here is a man who has already been saved by his faith in Christ, and Christ has already died for him. Yet we do not call him a brother, but instead a member of the "faction of unbelief." We are accusing and cursing him before God, calling upon God to deny salvation to him, convicting him, and discriminating him from the heavenly kingdom. Who are we, daring to bear false testimony to hurt a person in front of God?" (*Tianfeng*, No. 12)

In reply, Wang Mingdao said:

> Let me solemnly inform Mr. Ding, the term "faction of unbelief" is not just an arbitrary label. It is intended for one kind of people. These people call themselves Christians, but do not believe Biblical truths that require faith on the part of the believers. For example, they do not believe that Man was directly created by God; they do not believe in the virgin birth of Christ; they do not believe that Jesus redeemed men from their sins on the cross; they do not believe in Jesus' bodily resurrection; and they do not believe that Jesus will come again. Yet they do not state their unbelief clearly. Instead, they use vague expressions to disguise their unbelief. When necessary, they will even say that they believe these truths. But, "there is nothing concealed that will not be disclosed, or hidden that will not be made known" (Luke 12:2). Since they do not believe, they will not be able to hide their true views forever. Whoever belongs to this category is by definition a member of the "faction of unbelief." How can the use of this term be accused as engaging in "arbitrary labeling"? It is not the first time this term has been used. I first used it 26 years ago to describe such kinds of people... It is unreasonable to accuse us of using the term to "accuse and condemn others before God." It is not intended to "accuse and condemn others," but simply stating a fact! The apostle Paul himself actually used the following serious words: "I am astonished that you are so quickly deserting the one who called you by the grace of Christ and are turning to a different gospel—which is really no gospel at all. Evidently some people are throwing you into confusion and are trying to pervert the gospel of Christ. But even if we or an angel from heaven should preach a gospel other than the one we preached to you, let him be eternally condemned! As we have already said, so now I say again: If anybody is preaching to you a gospel other than what you accepted, let him be eternally condemned!" (Galatians 1:6-9)

There were some in the Galatian church who preached that only those who obeyed the Law and were circumcised could be saved. Paul referred to this message as "a different gospel." He also condemned it on God's behalf. The doctrine of the modernists, when compared with those who advocate salvation through keeping the Law and circumcision, is even more absurd, more contrary to God's word, and more destructive of people's faith. If Mr. Ding is so concerned on just hearing the term "faction of unbelief," I wonder what he feels when reading the above-mentioned passage. (Mingdao 1955)

Historical events are sometimes surprisingly similar! Not long ago, Ding made another speech on the issue of faction of unbelief, similar to what he had said in the 1950s. He said,

Some individuals, because of a difference in theological views, wantonly label others as the "faction of unbelief." As the church's self-appointed policemen, they cut off the means of earning a living of those pastors and co-workers who hold different views. This is unethical and lacking in love. Who gave us the authority to judge which persons belong to the "faction of unbelief" thus being a false believer and deserving excommunication? (*Tianfeng*, January 2000)

Of course, Wang Mingdao is no longer alive to answer Ding's question. But the kind of spirit that he possessed "to contend for the faith that was once for all entrusted to the saints" (Jude, verse 3) continues to exist in today's church. The truth of the Bible is still the ultimate measuring stick to judge all false teaching in the church whether past, present, or future.

As the chief representative of today's modern theological thought in China, Ding may have improved his ability to express himself, compared to his predecessors. However, the substance of their basic unbelief is the same. In the past, such modernists as Wu Yaozong (the first leader of the Protestant TSPM in the 1950s and 1960s) clearly expressed their basic unbelief. Wu stated quite blatantly that "all Christian doctrines that could be directly or indirectly drawn from the Bible," such as the Incarnation, the Virgin Birth, the Resurrection, the Trinity, the Last Judgement, and the Second Coming etc are "absurd, fantastic and incomprehensible beliefs." "No matter how hard I forced myself, I could never accept them" (Yaozong).

But Ding expresses himself more subtly. He states: The fundamental belief of the church...cannot be changed," however, "theological thought" can undergo "appropriate adjustments." For instance, "we strongly believe that Christ accomplished the task of reconciling God and Man while on the cross. However, we are unable to express clearly how that was actually accomplished. There are many different theological interpretations." It is important to "distinguish properly fundamental beliefs from theological thinking.

But how does one make this distinction? Ding believes that you can hold on to the fundamental belief that Christ died on the cross for all people. Yet, at the same time, you can also maintain the theological thinking that "those who do not believe in Christ will also finally enjoy eternal salvation." This is what he means by *proper distinctions*. According to Ding, this proper distinction is "a major development in theological research" by the Three-Self Patriotic Movement over the past ten years. It is due to "guidance of the church by the Holy Spirit." ("The Inevitability of Adjustments in Theological Thought," *Tianfeng*, March 2000.)

This is surely very deceptive. One's theological thought certainly reflects one's basic belief, and is one's interpretation of that belief. The two are inseparable. Ding's proper distinction is nothing less than an attempt to use his theological thought to deny and destroy the basic faith of the Chinese church. To call his introduction of false theology as being due to the guidance of the Holy Spirit is close to blasphemy. The Spirit of God is the Spirit of truth, who leads the church into the truth—not away from it (John 16:13). Ding's development over half a century of Wu Yaozong's modernist theology, merely added a more attractive veneer which is both more paradoxical and more deceptive. With this understanding, the reader may perceive what a theological milestone Ding's *Essays* is and what kind of epochal meaning the book has for the history of Christianity in China.

Ding's *Essays* are a combination of many different thoughts and perspectives (see Appendix One of this book). He mixes together Marxist dialectical materialism, his own imaginary religious Communism, liberal theology, as well as his re-interpretation of the sociological perspectives of Wu Yaozong, and his subjective interpretations of the theology of Teilhard de Chardin, process theology and liberation theology. One can see the gradual process by which he formed his ecclesiology based on Three-Self and supported by the political power of the Party. In this mixture, some ideas were taken by him without any change while others were developed by him. Sometimes he uses de Chardin's words to say what he wants to say—at other times he lets Alfred North Whitehead[1] speak for him. When he needs evidence to support his view of "the Cosmic Christ," Ding states that de Chardin had already talked about this idea. When Ding seeks to formulate his own view of God he states that Whitehead's God fascinated him. Many passages in Ding's *Essays* cleverly use the ideas of other theologians and philosophers to express his own subtle meaning.

Because the *Essays* do contain some elements of Christian faith, we cannot simply view them as only treatises on political or social theories. Yet, because they are filled with secular, political and cultural perspectives, we cannot treat them simply as theology either. Ding's thought is merely the product of a politico-religious figure that emerged from a particular environment, for the purpose of "accommodating" God's word to human Communist "ideology." Ding's "accommodation" is heartfelt thoroughly misleading because in actuality, Chinese Communism is his "basic belief" and "ultimate concern. " In the *Essays*, Ding does not openly admit his belief in Communism, but he indirectly describes it as "the community of mankind according to God's will" or "a higher faith" (*Essays*, p. 213 and 109. Ding is clearly aware of his peculiar status. He can easily find his "position" on China's "socio-political map" (*Essays*, p. 108). In his *Essays* Ding strives to find a theological basis for his "basic belief"—which is basically Marxist

However, since Ding's *Essays* are regarded by some as a "milestone in Chinese theology," we will analyze them from a biblical and theological perspective. We will discuss Ding's view of God, Christology, his view of Man, his theory of salvation, ecclesiology, and view of the Bible. If certain political comments are unavoidable, this is due to the intimate relationship between Ding's "theological thought" and Chinese official ideology.

Notes

1. Alfred North Whitehead (1861-1947) was an English Christian theologian who was a representative figure of process theology.

2

Ding's View of God

Let us first ask whether Mr. Ding has ever had a biblical view of God as his faith has evolved? The answer given by his *Essays* is negative. In an essay entitled, "A Chinese Christian's View of God," Ding provides some very severe self-criticism. He said that his early training caused him at one point to imagine "an omnipotent, self-existing, independent, unchanging God who possessed enormous power and authority" (*Essays*, p. 107). At that time he "acknowledged that there was a loving God, but love was not God's greatest attribute, being overshadowed by his righteousness, severity, anger, judgment, and arbitrariness" (*Essays*, p. 107). "Our education has led us to imagine a God who, as the highest authority, has the power to either condemn us to hell or raise us to the clouds" (*Essays*, p. 112). He admitted that the God in his early years was created with his imagination through the images of the rulers in ancient Egypt, Persia, Rome, and China; he assigned the attributes of the Pharaohs and Caesars to Him. Now he wants to "set aside all the attributes that man ascribed to Him, including His absolute authority, absolute knowledge, His unchangingness, absolute rule, arbitrariness, and intolerance," because "these attributes actually only reflect the desires of human beings, especially male" (*Essays*, p. 112).

If Ding's admission about the faith of his earlier years is honest—in other words, if Ding truly believed (Ding uses the word imagination to describe his faith) in the God he described—then we may say that Ding has never had a view of God that is in harmony with biblical revelation. Rather, we may say that he had a view of God that could only be shared by an atheist because he mixed God's attributes with images of human tyrants. In this regard, Ding's god is very similar to the German atheist Feuerbach's[1] God. Feuerbach said: "Our

God, though loving, is still a fierce god filled with religious fanaticism" (Feuerbach 1841, 91).

However, the problem does not stop there. Ding said that after years of toil, he moved toward "another kind of spiritual pursuit: To view the love of Christ manifested in the four gospels as God's essential attribute" (*Essays*, p. 107). Concerning this "spiritual pursuit," he states:

> Behind God's entire creative process is his love. Today, when I speak of Jesus Christ's revelation of God, I refer primarily to his revelation of God's love. In the past, I was enthusiastic about affirming Jesus' divine character. Today, I feel that it is more important to affirm God's loving character, like Christ's. For me, love is the first attribute of God. God is love. (*Essays*, p. 107)

Is it possible that, after moving toward another kind of spiritual pursuit, he suddenly woke up and wanted to accept the God revealed in the Bible? After all, the above passage contains such phrases as the "four gospels," "Christ's character of love" and "God is love."

Unfortunately not. On the contrary, the above passage reveals his intention to destroy the biblical view of God. Ding tries to use a conceptualized and crippled God to replace the true and living God revealed in the Bible, with the purpose of finding a "universal principle" for his "basic belief" which is Communism or his so-called "community of mankind according to God's will." Wu Yaozong, Ding's mentor and friend, once confessed to Premier Zhou Enlai[2] that he intended to harmoniously blend Christian theology with Communist philosophy, and that Marxism and Christianity were basically 99 percent in common and could eventually become one (Leung 1996, footnote p. 15). What Ding has been engaged in is simply Wu Yaozong's unfinished enterprise.

Is it wrong for Ding to temporarily put Jesus' deity on the back burner in order to affirm that God's Christ-like loving character is more important? We will discuss this question later. Let us first take a look at Ding's proposition that love is God's first attribute, as well as his motivation behind it.

The Bible indeed reveals that God is love (1 John 4:8, 16), God loves the world (John 3:16), love comes from God (1 John 4:7), and His love endures forever (this phrase occurs 26 times in Psalm 136). However, the Bible does not say that because God is love, so love is

God's first attribute. Verse one of Psalm 136 reads: "Give thanks to the Lord, for he is good." Only after proclaiming God's goodness did the poet joyfully shout, "His love endures forever." Does this mean that because goodness was listed before love therefore goodness is God's first attribute? Of course not. Similarly, God's proclamation on many occasions that "I am holy" (Leviticus 11:44, 45; 1 Peter 4:16) does not mean that holiness is necessarily God's first attribute. The book of Hebrews says that Jesus is "the radiance of God's glory and the exact representation of his being, sustaining all things by his powerful word" (Hebrews 1:3; this passage is often used by Ding to support his concept of "the Cosmic Christ"). This passage mentions God's *glory*, His *being*, or *existence*, and His powerful word. Which of the three is God's first attribute? Does it mean that the powerful word which sustains all things is superior to his glory and his existence and thus becomes God's first attribute? Hermeneutics would certainly deny this kind of theological deduction. God does not have a first attribute or a last attribute. God has multiple attributes harmoniously united.

However, Ding insists that, "Love is God's highest attribute, exceeding all other attributes, so that all other attributes become secondary;" (*Essays*, p. 102) "God's fundamental attribute is not his omnipotence, his omniscience, nor his 'self-existence,' but his 'love'" (*Essays*, p. 20). "To recognize that God is love is to recognize that God's highest attribute does not lie in his omnipotence, his omniscience, his 'I AM THAT I AM,' his majesty, authority and power, all of which are God's attributes, but not his most essential attribute" (*Essays,* p. 87). Elsewhere, Ding refers to God as "the model of the highest form of existence in the universe." "The first attribute of this highest form of existence is not any of his other attributes that overwhelm people such as his omnipotence, omniscience, omnipresence, 'I AM THAT I AM,' majesty, and authority and power; it is his everlasting love" (*Essays*, p. 272). "Love is God's most fundamental attribute; love is the basic attribute of this universe" (*Essays*, p. 260).

The God revealed in the Bible is a perfect God (Matthew 5:48). God's perfection is manifested through the completeness and indivisibility of his attributes. Theologians theologically divided God's attributes into holiness, kindness, goodness, righteousness, omniscience, omnipotence, omnipresence, everlasting being, etc., for the sake of convenience in presentation. No Bible-respecting theologian would arbitrarily uplift a certain attribute of God over others, because God's attributes are mutually-regulating, mutually-complementary, and mutually-affirming. It is impossible to discuss the so-called first attribute of love by separating it from God's holiness, righteousness, mercy, faithfulness, truthfulness, and goodness because this type of "love" does not exist. It is even more mistaken to treat the attribute of "I AM THAT I AM" (Exodus 3:14), which reveals God's existence and eternal nature, as a derivative of love—the so-called first attribute. The God revealed in the Bible is one who exists eternally. He has life, love, kindness, and righteousness in Himself. God is not one who exists because he loves. There is not one element of God's attribute that is more substantial than the others because every one is basic to His nature.

A tripod must have three legs in the same length to keep it balanced. If one of the three legs is cut short or made longer, the tripod can't stand, it will fall down. Ding tried to destroy the biblical view of God in the same way. A theologian once pointed out, "In the study of God's attributes it is important not to exalt one attribute over another; when that is done it presents a caricature of God. It is all the attributes of God taken together that provide an understanding of the nature and person of God" (Enns 1989, 188). Naturally, Ding is not satisfied with simply presenting a caricature of God. He must create a god to serve his basic [Marxist] belief. Having noticed the biblical proclamation that God is love, he realizes that he might succeed more readily if he were to distort the divine love. Seeing the uproar he has caused in the Chinese Christian community by his *Essays*, he appears to have already achieved this goal to a certain degree.

At this point, it is necessary to examine the content of the love considered by Ding to be God's first attribute. A casual reader might believe that Ding found the meaning of God's love through a complete reading of the Bible. But, in reality, the *Essays* studiously avoid expressing the true meaning of *agape*, the divine love.

The primary meaning of *agape* is to sacrifice out of goodness, so that the recipient may have benefit and joy. The biblical teaching that God is love means that God has sacrificed his Son in order to remove God's wrath brought about because of Man's sin and to give life to those who accept His Son.

The Bible has expressed the attribute of God's love and its relevance to human beings in John 3:16: "God so loved the world that he gave his one and only Son, that whoever believes in him shall not perish but have eternal life."

This passage tells us that God, being love, sacrificed His own Son and gave Him for sinners whom He loves and wants to save. God's attribute of love requires the loved ones to accept his love by faith. The love of Jesus revealed in the four Gospels is precisely this kind of love. Through His incarnation, death on the cross, and resurrection, Jesus Christ historically and truthfully revealed God's love in both time and space. At the same time, he also revealed the fact that only through faith can human beings establish a living relationship with him and his love, to obtain his salvation (Matthew 8:10, 9:28-29, 17:17-20, 21:21; Mark 1:15, 4:40, 5:36, 10:52, 19:19; Luke 7:50, 8:48, 17:5-6; 17:19; 18:8, 23:42-43; 24:25; John 1:10-13, 3:10-21, 3:31-36, 5: 24-25, 6:35-58, 6:68, 8:23-24, 8:32-38, 9:35-38, 10:25-30, 11:25-27, 13: 19, 14:1-14, 21:31).

Ding claims that he respects the four Gospels. However, he often avoids the above-mentioned passages, because they speak of the living relationship between God and sinners and also the significance of faith. Ding once unexpectedly cited John 3:16. But he showed no interest in the second half of this passage.

Besides showing Jesus Christ's revelation of the attribute of God's love, the New Testament also has given some very precise, clear, and concrete explanations of God's love. The book of Romans says:

> But God demonstrates his own love for us in this: While we were still sinners, Christ died for us. Since we have now been justified by his blood, how much more shall we be saved from God's wrath through him! For if, when we were God's enemies, we were reconciled to him through the death of his Son, how much more, having been reconciled, shall we be saved through his life! (Romans 5:8-10)

The first Epistle of John, which proclaims that God is love, explains love this way: "This is how God showed his love among us: He sent his one and only Son into the world that we might live through him. This is love: not that we loved God, but that he loved us and sent his Son as an atoning sacrifice for our sins" (1 John 4:9-10).

"This is how we know what love is: Jesus Christ laid down his life for us. And we ought to lay down our lives for our brothers" (1 John 3:16).

"And this is his command: to believe in the name of his Son, Jesus Christ, and to love one another as he commanded us" (1 John 3:23).

"And so we know and rely on the love God has for us. God is love. Whoever lives in love lives in God, and God in him. In this way, love is made complete among us so that we will have confidence on the Day of Judgment, because in this world we are like him" (1 John 4:16-17).

"To him who loves us and has freed us from our sins by his blood..." (Rev. 1:5).

It is very clear from Scripture that God's love is supremely expressed in the atonement of Christ on the cross.

After comparing the love of Christ defined by these Bible passages with the love of Christ mentioned in the *Essays*, we discovered that Ding's statement, "We must allow the love of Christ to become a definition of God and the highest revelation of God's essence" (*Essays* p. 97), was simply deceptive. Naturally, Ding does not want the love of Christ as expressed in the Bible to become the definition of God, because this is the kind of God that he had tried very hard to deny. Once departing from God's revelation, we would have no knowledge or understanding of God's attributes. Apart from the Bible's definition of *agape*, the love of which we speak is no longer an attribute of God. When Ding ignores God's revelation and the perfect teachings of the Bible, the first attribute of love that he ascribes to God simply becomes an empty universal principle, an essential attribute of the universe and the essence of the universal creation. This kind of voice can be heard in the philosophies of Pantheism and Panentheism, but not in the Bible.

Ding has not only distorted God's attribute of love, he has also misinterpreted other attributes of God. For example, God's justice is distorted beyond recognition. What is God's justice? Ding says: "God's justice is still God's love. When love is popularized among the masses or has entered the world, it becomes justice" (*Essays*, p. 56). "I would not say that God's highest attribute is his justice. Justice is derived from love. To talk about God's justice apart from God's love will result in a twisted religion, which would view God as a master who rewards the good and punishes the evil" (*Essays*, p. 102).

According to Ding, a God who rewards good and punishes evil is the product of a twisted religion, for in a normal religion, God's righteousness does not include rewarding good and punishing evil, but only spreading love to the masses (*Essays*, p. 102). In Ding's view, if you preach that: your God is "a consuming fire, a jealous God" (Deuteronomy 4:24; Hebrews 12:29); the "wrath of God is being revealed from heaven against all the godlessness and wickedness of men who suppress the truth by their wickedness" (Romans 1:18); "when the Lord Jesus is revealed from heaven in blazing fire with his powerful angels, he will punish those who do not know God and do not obey the gospel of our Lord Jesus" (2 Thessalonians 1:7-8); the judgment before the great white throne will certainly take place; then you are over-emphasizing God's justice apart from God's love, and your religion is a twisted religion.

God's justice and love, as revealed in the Bible, are mutually-defined and mutually enforcing.

> Thus, justice is loving justice and love is just love.... If love does not include justice, it is mere sentimentality.... Actually, love and justice have worked together in God's dealing with man. God's justice requires that there be payment of the penalty for sin. God's love, however, desires man to be restored to fellowship with him. The offer of Jesus Christ as the atonement for sin means that both the justice and the love of God have been maintained. And there really is not tension between the two. There is tension only if one's view of love requires that God forgive sin without any payment being made (Erickson, p. 298).

Not only has Ding divided God's attributes of love and justice, he has also belittled God's other attributes. He repeatedly points out that God's justice, power and authority, omniscience, omnipotence, etc. are merely God's affiliated, secondary, or derived attributes. In particular, these attributes reminded him of Caesar, the ruler of hell, and human tyrants. Believers who preach these attributes are under his rebuke. He said, "For a long time, our church never spoke of God's love as his highest attribute but spoke of his power and fearsome control....the result of such preaching is that Christians come to view non-Christians with hostility, as Jonah viewed the people of

Nineveh" (*Essays*, p. 85). I would like to ask Ding how many people can you find among the tens of millions of Chinese Christians who do not speak of God's love but only God's wrath, and view non-Christians with hostility?

Ding has distorted the biblical view of God's love. Next, I would like to ask in his own words: "What precisely causes this person to raise this kind of proposition? What problem does he hope to resolve?" (*Essays*, p. 188).

To answer these questions, we must first locate Mr. Ding's "position in the socio-political map of China" (*Essays*, p. 108). When we discuss the socio-political role that he has played, we are not referring to his being a beneficiary of the political system. (Although it is clear that he attained a high official position in both the National People's Congress and People's Political Consultative Committee and is living, by Chinese standards, luxuriously and has been designated by Chinese government as the "leader and spokesman of Chinese Christianity." Consequently, he can exercise his official right to interpret the Bible in the "religious community," within China and even abroad. He can also use the political power to forcibly propagate his theological thinking.) No, I am not referring to these things, but to his political views expressed in the *Essays* and in the relationship between them and his view of God. I refer to the motivation which lies behind his view of God

In the article entitled "A Chinese Christian's View of God," Ding made the following emotional comments, while maintaining a firm political position:

> My belief in God's love and my belief that China should go the socialist way are compatible and mutually reinforcing. Socialism uses love to organize the masses... I firmly believe that, for China, feudalism, colonialism, and capitalism cannot replace what we refer to as socialism with Chinese characteristics... From the perspective of a long history, I do not believe that socialism is a detour in the path of mankind or an accidental phenomenon that can be erased now... We place our hope in socialism not because we have seen its detailed blueprint; but because no other choice has captured our imagination (*Essays*, p. 108).

> There are some who espouse atheism. Does this fact affect my support for socialism? No...I know many atheists, who are working honestly and diligently to create a more humane society. Their de-

nial of God is in reality an affirmation of humanity. Their atheism is a criticism of the mistaken view of God that has been propagated by those in the religious communities. Every one of their criticisms is worthy of our sympathy. What kind of God have these people denied? It is an autocratic Zeus, who chained Prometheus to a mountain because Prometheus obtained seeds of fire in order to raise Man's quality of life. It is an autocratic ruler of hell, who sent his messengers to toss people who have made mistakes into the eternal fire of hell as a punishment. Atheists who preach humanism as a means of seeking a higher meaning to life may be our allies in the development of a superior faith (*Essays,* p. 109).

These words are definitely songs in praise of Socialism and atheism which the socialists and atheists themselves could not express better. Hidden in these comments is an outline of Ding's own basic faith; by insisting on Socialism, through him and his atheist allies' humanist efforts, one attains a superior faith, that is, Communism.

Mr. Ding is a sober, highly self-conscious, and religious type of Communist. This type of person is rare in China. His religious training has allowed him to notice Communism's·deficiencies (such as the lack of love). His complete loyalty to Communism requires him to shrewdly absorb some religious beliefs into his basic ideology. He knows that both God and Christianity can be used in the process of attaining this superior faith, (In his *Essays,* he often repeats these concepts for the benefit of his atheist allies.) Under these circumstances, Whitehead's God is used to support Ding's God, and de Chardin's unbiblical eschatology provides an explanation for Ding's Communism. Ding remarked that "human beings are more capable of comprehending" de Chardin's eschatology because de Chardin viewed the end times as "the beginning of a new historical stage" after the realization of "the human community." De Chardin provided "moving prophecies" of that "new historical stage:" "On that day, after we are able to control wind and rain, tides and waves, and gravity, we shall control the energy of love for God. At that time, mankind shall be as if they have just discovered the seed of fire for the second time in world history" (*Essays,* p. 203).

Ding further explains: "To re-discover the seed of fire means that mankind can fully control and exploit the energy of love, and thus can exercise self-governance and self-management" (*Essays,* p. 114, 203). Ding believes that when mankind can handle the universal principle of love to engage in self-governance and self-management they can then claim the attributes of God as their own. They can thus replace God, who can then retreat from the history of mankind. Evolution will then have been completed, and God—whether he is the autocratic dictator or the god of love—will finally retire from the stage.

Ding seems to have forgotten the biblical warning given in the history of the Tower of Babel, which is God's judgment on human pride and arrogance. Beneath his Christian veneer, his passion for Communism keeps peeking through. The effort to construct a human community in rebellion against God appeared long ago in human history as recorded in the book of Genesis: "Come, let us build ourselves a city, with a tower that reaches to the heavens, so that we may make a name for ourselves and not be scattered over the face of the whole earth" (Genesis 11:4).

But, because of God's intervention, mankind's effort to create a community that would not be scattered over the face of the whole earth has failed. However, this rebellious consciousness has continued until now, being deeply ingrained in man's sinful nature. This is precisely the kind of consciousness that Ding appears to express through his basically humanist and Marxist view of God.

Notes

1. Ludwig Andreas Feuerbach (1804-1872) was the source of ideas that had significant influence on Karl Marx and Friedrich Engels, who drew from Feuerbach the belief that the material realm is the basis for all ideology. Later, Marx criticized Feuerbach for not making a clean break with Hegel.

2. Zhou Enlai (1898-1976) was the premier of the People's Republic of China before his death.

3

Ding's View of God (Continued)

Ding's view of God has been in continuous development. In an article entitled "The Progressive Nature of Revelation," Ding claimed that this developing view of God could "be used to harmonize the so-called contradictions in the Bible" (*Tianfeng*, 1999, special issue). The viewpoint contained in this article supplements his view of God expressed in his *Essays*.

Ding gives considerable thought to the title of this article so that it might give a clear impression that he was talking about the progressive nature of revelation. In other words, "God's revelation in the Bible was progressive and was not completed immediately. So was Man's understanding of God's revelation" (*Tianfeng*, 1999, special issue). If we look only at the title of his article we might almost agree with him, for indeed biblical revelation *was* progressive. A correct view of revelation tells us that the entire Bible is the authoritative record of God's revelation. From the Old Testament to the New Testament, God progressively revealed his plan of salvation, as the author of Hebrews said: "In the past God spoke to our forefathers through the prophets at many times and in various ways, but in these last days he has spoken to us by his Son, whom he appointed heir of all things, and through whom he made the universe" (Hebrews 1:1-2).

However, Ding does not honor this view of revelation. In his view, the reason that God's revelation is progressive is because God needs to use later revelations to negate his earlier ones. He needs to continuously "correct" the mistakes made by people who received God's revelations, including Moses, Joshua, Jonah, and certain Psalmists. To us who respect the Bible, these individuals were prophets chosen by God to record his revelations and to transmit his messages.

But to Ding, the view of God transmitted by them was barbaric and inhumane. Ding said, "Many examples of this view of God were recorded in Deuteronomy, Joshua, and other [Old Testament books]" (*Tianfeng*, 1999 special issue). By using the term "others," Ding obviously wanted to tell his readers that this view of God was also contained in other Old Testament books, such as the Psalms.

In order to show the barbaric and inhumane nature of this view of God, Ding cited such scriptures as Deuteronomy 20:16-17, Joshua 10:40, Psalm 137:9. However, not only do these passages not help him to achieve his objective, but they also expose his true intention to deny Biblical revelation. Let us use Deuteronomy 20:16-18 to examine the degree to which Ding has distorted the view of God as revealed in Scripture.

The three verses of Deuteronomy 20:16-18 cannot be arbitrarily lifted out of context without damaging their meaning. Verses 16 and 17 state:

> However, in the cities of the nations the Lord your God is giving you as an inheritance, do not leave alive anything that breathes. Completely destroy them—the Hittites, Amorites, Canaanites, Perizzites, Hivites and Jebusites—as the Lord your God has commanded you.

Please observe that Ding appears to stop here deliberately, without quoting verse 18 that provides the rationale for God's command that they be completely destroyed, which is "otherwise, they will teach you to follow all the detestable things they do in worshiping their gods, and you will sin against the Lord your God." This verse completely nullifies Ding's criticism of God's being barbaric and inhumane in Deuteronomy. These verses also express God's attribute of holiness, the plan and purpose of his election, and his hatred of sin.

The thoughts in Deuteronomy 20:16-18 are intimately tied to the overall theme of the Pentateuch. Without a covenant between God and Abraham, as recorded in Genesis 15:18-21, there would have been no statement like "the Lord your God is giving you as an inheritance." Without God's hatred and judgment of the sins of the Canaanites, as recorded in Leviticus, the command to completely destroy them would not have appeared in these verses. Leviticus 18:1-5 states:

The Lord said to Moses, "Speak to the Israelites and say to them: 'I am the Lord your God. You must not do as they do in Egypt, where you used to live, and you must not do as they do in the land of Canaan, where I am bringing you. Do not follow their practices. You must obey my laws and be careful to follow my decrees.... for the man who obeys them will live by them. I am the Lord.'"

The next 18 verses (6-23) give a list of the Canaanites' sinful ways which include all kinds of adultery and the sin of sacrificing children by fire to false gods. Then, God said to Moses:

Do not defile yourselves in any of these ways, because this is how the nations that I am going to drive out before you became defiled. Even the land was defiled; so I punished it for its sin, and the land vomited out its inhabitants. But you must keep my decrees and my laws.... and do not follow any of the detestable customs that were practiced before you came and do not defile yourselves with them. I am the Lord your God. (Leviticus 18:24-30; Deuteronomy 12:29-31)

Jehovah's decrees and laws were encapsulated in the Ten Commandments, which is the common standard by which God judged his chosen people and the Gentiles alike. The Bible told us that God had previously judged and condemned the Canaanites who had practiced "detestable, sinful ways." All Moses did was merely to carry out the Lord's command to completely destroy them, so that God's people would not be defiled by the sinful ways that offended God. Likewise, what Joshua did was part of a series of events "just as the Lord, the God of Israel, had commanded" (Joshua 10:40).

The Pentateuch and the book of Joshua record many occasions in which God's servants acted as God commanded. From Noah (Genesis 6:22) to Abraham (Genesis 12:4, 17:23), from Moses to Joshua, acting as God commanded became a continuous expression of their obedience to God. When Moses did not act as God commanded only once, God did not permit him to enter the land of Canaan with the other Israelites (Numbers 20:7-12). Therefore, the two phrases "as the Lord your God commanded you" and "just as the Lord, the God of Israel, had commanded" recorded in Deuteronomy 20:16-18 and Joshua 10:40, respectively, are definitely not statements that can be ignored or discarded, for they are evidence of God's revelation and commands.

If Ding questions the revelatory factor in these passages, he certainly may also disbelieve the reliability of all the other historical events recorded in the Bible, which took place as a result of the Lord's command. If what Moses and Joshua had done as commanded by the Lord were barbaric and inhumane, then, in Ding's view, God's decisions to "destroy the earth" through the flood during Noah's time (Genesis 6:13-17) and to burn down Sodom and Gomorrah with burning sulphur during Abraham's time (Genesis 19:24) must have been even more barbaric and inhumane.

Statements such as "the Lord commanded," "the Lord said to Moses," and "the Lord's words came down..." appear 3,800 times in the Old Testament. They have equal effect when used to express God's revelation and commands. To deny the authority and reliability of any one of them is to deny the authority and reliability of the entire Old Testament.

Ding does not uphold the orthodox view of the inspiration of the Bible. He seems to disdain the truth that "all Scripture is given by the inspiration of God" (2 Timothy 3:16, KJV). He has no intention to respect the authority and integrity of biblical revelation. On the contrary, Ding likes to examine and then to judge the Bible. He can then set himself up as arbiter and point out which parts of Scripture were the Israelites' "incorrect understanding of God" and which parts "could not have been the will of God." (*Tianfeng* 1999).

Having judged the Bible, the next logical step is to judge God. Therefore we should not be surprised by his humanistic statements which he has determined himself. The *Essays* are full of judgments of God. Ding attacks God as "the autocratic Zeus" (p. 109); "the Caesar who rules over all" and "the severe and cruel moralist" (p. 111 and 231); "the God who acts like a bulldozer" (p. 112); "a vengeful, fearful, totalitarian God" (p. 97); "the God who is so politically reactionary" (p. 140); "a dishonest God" (p. 144); "a ruler of hell" (p. 149); and "the view that God is unchanging...can no longer stand on solid ground" (p. 231). Aside from these "judgments," he also has some positive things to say about "God." For example, God is the "force that constantly is creating goodness" (p. 151); "our God is so generous and loving, he would not toss people into hell just because they do not believe in him" (p. 288). Ding's descriptions are based on a scornful attitude toward the biblical revelation.

In the *Essays* and the article "The Progressive Nature of Revelation," Ding attempted to use his view of revelation to explain his view of God. However, in doing so, and because of the falsity of his view of revelation, he made his view of God even more absurd. The discussion of the progressive nature of revelation in Christian theology is normally based on the presupposition that revelation is harmonious. Apart from this presupposition, one could certainly make incorrect deductions based on the progressive nature of revelation. For example, some one might believe that later revelation negates earlier revelation, and that the New Testament revelation negates the Old Testament revelation. The progressive nature of revelation actually refers to the steps by which God carries out his plan of salvation. It refers to the historical development of God's mystery—Jesus Christ—in time and space "in order that they may know the mystery of God, namely, Christ" (Colossians 2:2). Christ's lordship in creation, salvation, and judgment, and His life, death, resurrection, and return are the focus of all biblical revelation.

Yet the progressive nature of the revelations understood by Ding is exactly the opposite of this vital truth. Ding believes that the progressive nature of revelation refers to God's effort to continuously reveal his character in the order of the various books in the Bible (from the earliest to the latest, from the lowest to the highest, etc.). He appears to believe that the authors of Deuteronomy and Joshua, owing to their inability to receive the revelation that God is love, misunderstood God, and thus created and upheld a barbaric and inhumane view of God; that some Psalmists and the prophet Jonah were also supporters of this view of God; and that almost the entire Old Testament is an "accumulative" record of the "Israelites' misunderstandings of God." "Finally," Ding said,

> In 1 John 4:16, we read that "God is love." We may believe that this point represents the zenith of the revelation of God in the Bible or the zenith in Man's understanding of God. God recognized that after a period of 1,000 years, from Deuteronomy, to Joshua, to the first book of John, man had reached a sufficient level to receive the revelation that God is love; then he revealed this simple truth through the first book of John. In other words, only after such a long time would there be individuals who could understand, accept, and bear such a simple view of God, i.e., God is love. (*Tienfeng*, 1999)

But is it true that during the thousand years from Deuteronomy,

Joshua, to the first book of John God could not reveal His attribute of love because of man's inability to comprehend? Of course not! As early as in the book of Exodus, God had already completely revealed His attributes to Moses:

> And he passed in front of Moses, proclaiming, "The Lord, the Lord, the compassionate and gracious God, slow to anger, abounding in love and faithfulness, maintaining love to thousands, and forgiving wickedness, rebellion and sin. Yet he does not leave the guilty unpunished. (Exodus 34:6-7)

In this revelation of God's attributes, God's love, is mentioned twice and is described as abundant and for thousands. This biblical view of God is not as simple as Ding's view of God, for it encompasses God's grace, love, and compassion, as well as God's holiness, righteousness, and wrath. However, it is a complete and perfect revelation of God's attributes. It is absolutely impossible that Moses, who had received God's revelation on Mount Sinai and walked with God for 40 years, should form an incorrect view of God, and then through inspiration record it in the book of Deuteronomy. Nor was it possible that the prophet Jonah, (who is repeatedly rebuked by Ding), not to have a God-inspired view of God (see Jonah 4:2). It goes without saying that throughout Psalms and other books in the Old Testament one can easily notice the descriptions of God's love. Yet, Ding chose to ignore all these passages and exaggerates that he has finally found that God is love only in 1 John, and proclaims that this represents the "zenith" of God's revealed character.

It is common knowledge among Christians that the zenith of God's revelation of his attributes (kindness, righteousness, holiness, power, etc.) is the cross. God manifested His love through the birth, death and resurrection of His son, Jesus Christ. The declaration in 1 John that "God is love" only restated the meaning of this revelation (please read carefully 1 John 4:8-18). In fact, in the gospel of John which preceded 1 John chronologically, the apostle John had already powerfully declared the meaning of this event and the attribute of God's love. This biblical knowledge reveals the difficulties inherent in Ding's "zenith theory."

Ding could not have been seeing a zenith and a simple view of God only after he nearly finished reading the entire Bible. He intends to destroy the authority of the Bible and the integrity of God's revelation, while seeking a seemingly truthful theological basis for his view of God, in order to confuse and destroy the biblically revealed view of God. Ding formulated his view of God through humanistic thought processes and by plucking Bible passages out of context. This theological method, which is limited by his own basic belief system, inevitably causes his view of God to be antibiblical.

4

Ding's Christology

1. The Origin of Ding's Christology

The basic content of Ding's theory of Christ is the "Universal Christ" or the "Cosmic Christ." This theory of Christ and his view of God constitute the two sides of Ding's theological thought: The Universal Christ responds to the universal principle of "God is love". Without further theoretical development, the universal principle would show its emptiness. Thus his proposal of a Universal Christ is quite natural.

The idea of a Universal Christ or Cosmic Christ was not invented by Ding. In 1820s, some German theologians began to use the concept of Cosmic Christ to discuss Cosmic nature of Christology. The idea came into English world after 1850's. The discussion was based on Jesus' divine nature and within the revelation of the Bible. Theologians before De Chardin such as A. M. Fairbarin, James Denny, G. B. Stevens and W. R. Inge all adopted this concept. It first appeared in Teilhard de Chardin's dairy on March 13, 1916. De Chardin provided additional explanations for this idea in his 1920 thesis entitled "Note on the Universal Christ" and 1924 article entitled "My Universe" and some subsequent works. What Ding has done is to "link it with the practical happenings in the Chinese revolution." This "link" allows Ding to visualize a "greater" Christ. He exclaims joyfully, "What could be better than this?" (*Essays,* p. 84)

As early as 1984, Ding declared in a speech: "We are seeking a vital theory of Christ" (*Essays,* p. 18). In this searching process, he was "inspired by liberation theology, by de Chardin's theology, and process theology,"—in particular by de Chardin's idea of the Universal Christ. This inspiration helped him to step out of the framework of the traditional theory of Christ (and so, naturally, completely outside of the biblical framework, too.) Later in 1991, in another speech entitled the "Universal Christ," he published his "vital theory of Christ." This theory of Christ allows him to "transfer from a narrow Christ who is concerned only for Christian believers to a broader Christ who fills all" (*Essays*, p. 203). He thus set himself free from "a narrow theological view centered on redemption that differentiates believers from non-believers." For the narrow theological view, that is, the evangelical gospel truth, is actually the faith of the vast majority of Christians in China as even Ding himself has admitted.

First, we would like to use the information provided by Ding to examine why he has been so passionate about popularizing the idea of the Universal Christ in China. We would like to see what special Chinese characteristics he has imparted to this originally foreign idea. Ding's ideas are expressed primarily in the two articles entitled "The Universal Christ" and "How to View Truth, Goodness, and Beauty outside of Christianity" and scattered among other articles.

In "The Universal Christ," Ding said, "The impact historical reforms had on traditional beliefs is the cause of this idea." The "so-called historical reforms refer to the series of changes that took place in China around the time of the establishment of the People's Republic of China [in 1949]" (*Essays*, p. 90).

This hint by Ding deserves attention: he attributed the concept of the Universal Christ in the early 1990s to the historical reforms that occurred around 1949. This hint reminds us again of the important role of Marxism in Ding's discussions on faith.

Ding believes that these historical reforms in China, (quite outside of the Christian faith), had created an enormous humanist and moral impact, leading him to see that "in China, the new creature that Paul spoke of has already come, the difference being that this new creature is not within the church, but outside it" (*Essays*, p. 91). This phenomenon "created puzzlement and provoked additional thinking among Chinese Christians" because "for a long time, Christianity has always used the fall of man and man's lack of goodness as the reason to preach about sin and Christ the savior. However, the occurrence of many new phenomena and realities in the new China could not but bring about some Christians' reconsideration or even doubt about traditional beliefs" (*Essays*, p. 91).

According to Ding, three kinds of people appeared in the Chinese church as a result of the impact of the Communist revolution.

The first kind were the "students and good friends of Mr. Wu Yaozong" (*Essays,* p. 92). They acknowledged Jesus "only as a great teacher of morality and as a social reformist." "They discovered that the Revolution provided China with enormous and exciting results, whereas Christianity's ability to reform China seemed negligible." Therefore, they "left the church to join what they believed to be a stronger organization" [i.e. the Communist Party] (*Essays,* p. 92).

A second kind were those who remained in the church, because to them Christ still seemed attractive. They began to study the Bible anew, realizing that they needed to "open a new path" for their "new spiritual pursuit" (*Essays,* p. 93).

The last kind were those who were stubborn (*Essays,* p. 92). They "confined themselves to a small world, tirelessly resisting new things and new thoughts" (*Essays,* p. 92). "They only knew how to categorize people into believers and non-believers, and spent much time writing about faith or the lack of faith. They "tried to support and strengthen their own belief by diligently searching for the various evil traces of human behavior" (*Essays,* p. 92). Naturally, they could not be allowed to remain in the church under the new regime.

Ding does not tell us the fate of this group of people. Yet, historical records show that most of them were sent to prison or labor camps. Some lived through the ordeal, while others died there.

Among these people, the first kind are Ding's friends, and the third kind his enemies. He probably considers himself to belong to the second category, those who remained in the church. However, this conclusion may raise an important question: As Ding himself was a student and friend of Wu Yaozong, why did he not join a stronger organization but choose to remain in the church?

This question may have no answer for the time being. However, judging from Ding's theology as demonstrated in his *Essays,* by remaining in the church, he has done far more harm to the Chinese church than those who switched to a stronger organization.

Returning to Christology, alert readers may recognize that the attribution of the idea of the Universal Christ to the impact of historical reforms on traditional belief, though may have increased the theory's political and historical basis, does not have any theological persuasiveness. Ding's historical view is one that roams widely across time and space. In the 1990s, he searched the historical reforms of the 1950s for traces of the Universal Christ. The irony is that Ding never mentions the terrible persecution of the Chinese church during the dark interlude from the early fifties to the end of the Cultural Revolution. During that dark period the Chinese sky echoed with the cries of Jesus Christ through His persecuted people: "Saul! Saul! Why do you persecute me?" (Acts 22:7-8)

In Ding's theological thinking, Jesus the Nazarene is different from the Universal Christ. The Jesus of Nazareth in the Bible knows nothing of Ding's Universal Christ.

A common mistake among humanists is to state that historical reforms impacted traditional Christian belief, resulting in the bankruptcy of faith or leading to the creation of new belief. Nearly 2,000 years of church history demonstrates that no orthodox beliefs or church doctrines will succumb to a political power under the pressure of historical reforms and thus betray the Bible's authority or become a tool for a political power or its ideology. The religious reformation led by Martin Luther and John Calvin stood against the sacrifice of faith by the mixing of church and state; they called upon the church to return to God and God's Word.

In addition, when describing historical reforms, Ding confuses several Christian principles, which need to be clarified:

(1) No historical reform can produce what Paul called the new creature. Only those who are born again by the Holy Spirit are truly what Paul called the new creature;

(2) "Paul's understanding of man's nature" (*Essays,* p. 91) shows that man is sinful. Ding's attempt to resolve the problem of sin by regular, continuous criticism and self-criticism is not practicable;

(3) Christianity's "Proclamation of sin and Savior Christ based on Man's fall and lack of goodness" is in no way changed by "the phenomenon and new reality which emerged in New China."

2. The Springboard of Ding's Christology

The impact of historical reforms on traditional beliefs prompted Ding to conceive the ideology of the Universal Christ. Ding realized that he must add some theological explanations to this ideology, otherwise "most Chinese Christians could not accept such a strongly politically-inclined teaching" (*Essays,* p. 92). (These Christians are the stubborn individuals, Evangelicals who refuse at great cost to accept a politicized theology.) Thus he said, "For Chinese Christians, it is extremely important to recognize the universal nature of Christ" (*Essays*, p. 93) because the "Cosmic Christ" is "a fairly common theological trend" of the Chinese church over the past 40 years, and "a central point of view in the theological deliberation of the Chinese church" (*Essays*, p. 272). Ding declared that, in the theological deliberation process of the Chinese church, "we have gradually freed ourselves from minor debates about Christ's human and divine natures, and through the universal nature of Christ, obtained liberation, deepening and consolidating our theological ideology" (*Essays*, p. 273).

According to biblical revelation, the Universal Christ is quite a proper concept. The Old Testament book of Genesis (especially the first three chapters), Psalms, Isaiah, etc., and the New Testament books of John, Ephesians, Philippians, Colossians, Hebrews and Revelation all provide a strong foundation of truth for this theological way of thinking. However, the biblical truth regarding the Universal Christ is fundamentally different from the Universal Christ promoted by Ding, Teilhard de Chardin, and later, the New Age movement.

The Universal Christ revealed in the Bible is the Word that was with God in the beginning. "The Word was God"—"Through him all things were made; without him nothing was made that has been made" (John 1:1-3). "He is before all things, and in him all things hold together" (Colossians 1:17). "The Son is the radiance of God's glory and the exact representation of his being, sustaining all things by his powerful word" (Hebrews 1:3). From Scripture we know that Christ has a complete relationship with the universe through his power to create, redeem, judge, and renew. The concept of the Cosmic Christ provides a perspective to view Christ from His works in the universe. However, to insist that this cosmic nature of Christ is additional to his divine and human natures is to add something extra to Christ's character. This way of handling the doctrine is basically no different from that of the heretics who denied either the divine or the human nature of Christ throughout church history.

Yet, the evolutionary theologian Teilhard de Chardin believed that there is a "third nature of Christ," which is "neither divine nor human, but universal" (de Chardin 1978). This Christ who has the third nature is the universal element that permeates all things (de

Chardin 1968, 60). This Cosmic Christ is the "internal driving force" of the universe's evolution, and the perfect final point of the universe's evolution (the so-called "Omega Point") (de Chardin 1968, 54). In de Chardin's view, the Universal Christ is an evolutionary Christ. The evolutionary process of the universe is actually the formation process of Christ. Both are mutually dependent, in fact, evolution saved Christ (rendered Christ possible); Christ also saved evolution (without Christ evolution could not be completed).

Under such circumstances, the divine and human natures of Christ become insignificant because the universal nature has replaced his divine nature, thus rendering Christ an "impersonal core of the universe that pierces through the entire evolutionary process" (de Chardin 1968, 54). Even the incarnation of Christ was viewed in the framework of the theory of evolution by de Chardin. The incarnation is no longer significant in God's plan of salvation and in Christ's obtaining a perfect human nature. Mankind no longer needs faith to establish a relationship with Christ. The incarnate Christ is merely the *milieu* through which man may discover and realize his own divinity.

It so happened that this novel theory of Christ by de Chardin came to be used as a timely springboard for those who were eager to leap outside of the framework of biblical Christology. Before Ding, a group of theologians active in the New Age Movement had already got on this springboard. These individuals admired de Chardin greatly, calling him the father of the New Age Movement. According to a survey of New Age activists regarding whose ideas had the most influence on them, the majority indicated it was de Chardin (Livesey). The New Age Movement is in essence an outburst of secular humanism wrapped in a spiritual coating. Its infiltration into theology is intent on thoroughly overthrow the Biblical doctrines of Christ and man, leading its many followers into the terrible abyss of self-inflated egotism and narcissism.

David Spangler, a spokesman for the New Age Movement, once said the following, which represents the essence of New Age theology: "If we want to demonstrate what we have is better than the mainline Christian tradition, something unachievable by the old Christ, it must be a Cosmic Christ, a Universal Christ, and a New Age Christ" (Spangler 1981). He said that these ideas might liberate people from Christ's God-man dualism and related doctrines. Spangler's Christ was "a principle of the universe and a kind of spiritual existence, a characteristic injected into and manifested in all religions and philosophies that promote humanity and seek spiritual unity" (Spangler 1980).

The viewpoint of Matthew Fox, another leading New Age theologian, is even more astonishing. He claimed that every one of us is divine and thus can declare "I AM," as Christ had done. He claimed that Jesus became Christ because he was Christ-conscious; and that since Christ is the anointed one, we all are anointed, we all have the divine nature, and we all are "Cosmic Christs" (Fox 1988, 138). (In fact these are old heresies which Christians in the seventeenth century were very familiar with!) Fox emphasized the need to leave the Christianity of a personal savior and enter into a Christianity of the Cosmic Christ. He said that this Cosmic Christ would bring about a divine universe and a profound universal church; that all religions would merge into the Cosmic Christ; and that people could achieve all these things without Jesus of Nazareth. He proclaimed that the Universal Christ has arrived, but it is not Jesus of Nazareth who had been resurrected and uplifted, but rather the Cosmic Christ is inside every human being on earth" because everyone has a life similar to Christ's (Fox 1988, 138).

Like de Chardin, who preceded them, all New Age theologians try hard to seek biblical support for their theories. They all distort the Bible in order to achieve their objectives. After all, they realized that without some biblical support, the theory of the Cosmic Christ constructed solely out of the evolution of the universe and the uplifting of human nature would not have any theological value or market. However, it has not been easy for them to find help from the Bible to support their conclusions. To solve this dilemma, they reject the authority of biblical revelation and trample on the integrity of biblical truth. They seek to make the Bible appear contradictory and interpret biblical passages out of proper context, directing them wherever they please. This is what De Chardin, Spangler, and Fox did. The same is true with Ding, who has used the same springboard.

3. The Content of Ding's "Cosmic Christ"

In his theorizing, Ding imitated de Chardin and his followers. In practical application, however, he blazed his own trail. The reality of the Chinese Communist revolution (or so-called socialism with Chinese characteristics) requires a Universal Christ with Chinese characteristics to match. In this Christ, to emphasize the difference between belief and unbelief has to be condemned, and Christians and atheists must become "fellow travelers" (*Essays*, p. 143). Ding's Christ is "far greater than what we usually imagine... He took from mankind— both believers and non-believers, deists and atheists—what they had accomplished, not to destroy, but to elevate, perfect, bless, and present it to God—the father of all" (*Essays*, p. 143). From Ding's point of view, unless the "truth, goodness, and beauty of this Christ" are "excavated" from the revolutionary and atheistic masses (*Essays*, p. 144), he should not exist. If Christ must exist this way to meet Man's needs, then, as mentioned by Ding before, leaving detailed debate over the divine and human natures of Christ and recognizing his universal nature becomes the path Ding must tread in his theological deliberation.

What is the universal nature of Christ? In "The Universal Christ, " Ding has the following two statements: (1) "Christ's sovereignty, concern, and love extend throughout the whole universe;" (2) "Christ's sovereignty throughout the universe is love in essence" (*Essays*, p. 93).

These two statements are seemingly correct but actually are not. It is neither biblical nor logical for him to use them to explain Christ's having a universal nature in addition to his human and divine natures.

The *cosmos* or the entire universe refers to the existence of a creation, which is the object of the Creator's work. Jesus Christ reigns over the universe, "sustaining all things by his powerful word" (Hebrews 1:3), because he "is God" (John 1:1), because by his incarnation he became man (John 1:14, Philippians 2:6-11), because he "was declared with power to be the Son of God by his resurrection from the dead" (Romans 1:4), and because he thus possesses "all authority in heaven and on earth" (Matthew 28:18). Christ has therefore formed a relationship with the universe of Creator to creation, and of Sustainer to the sustained. (The universe does not cease its operation only because of Christ's maintenance). However, relationship is not the same as nature. Christ's nature remains fully God and fully Man.

What is then the universal nature of Christ in Ding's mind?

Please note the terms *universal* and *love* used by Ding. He gives special meanings to these two terms. Through these two terms and his definitions, it is not difficult to understand that Ding's so-called Cosmic Christ leads inevitably to a Christ of universal salvation. The Cosmic Christ is the Christ of universal salvation. This is the ultimate goal of all the theological deliberation in the *Essays*, whether subtly hinted at or openly stated.

We have already analyzed Ding's discussion of love in Chapter Two of this book, where we also pointed out that what he referred to as God's most essential attribute—love—was simply a kind of universal principle, the first universal element, the nature of the creation of the universe, and the essential attribute of the universe. This kind of love differs greatly from the divine love revealed in the Bible. Ding's God is merely a code word for the universe. If this kind of love were indeed God's first, foremost and most essential attribute, then the true and living God revealed in the Bible would become merely a carrier of this universal principle, the internal driving force of the evolution of the universe, or simply be the universe itself. Once the triune God is eliminated from the universe, in the sky of religion one may see occasionally some fleeting cloud of false universal salvation or hear some empty rhetoric of love by Ding and others like him.

If God is this kind of universal manifestation, then Christ cannot but be a Universal Christ. If love is an essential attribute of the universe, then the universal nature of Christ must be one of universal salvation. Now, the essence of Ding's theory of the Cosmic Christ has emerged. The theory of universal salvation is his greatest theological concern.

According to the universalists, all human beings will be saved ultimately whether they believe in Jesus or not. The great contemporary evangelist John R. W. Stott has forcefully pointed out that universal salvation is "Satan's lie." Many will be deceived by this lie and as a result lose the opportunity to accept Jesus and obtain eternal life. This lie echoes Satan's lie in the Garden of Eden, "You will be like God..." (Genesis 3:5). The earlier lie destroyed the relationship between Man and God, which had been established by God's creation, leading man to fall into sin and ultimately death. This later lie is aimed at damaging God's redemption centered on the cross of

Christ, causing many to refuse to accept Christ's salvation by faith and thus suffer eternal punishment.

Ding's theological deliberations provide proof for universalism in three main respects. First, since God's highest attribute is his love, "he would not toss people into hell just because they do not believe in him" (*Essays,* p. 288). Second, the universal nature of Christ would prompt him to "extend his salvation to the masses," and "Christ would save not only Christians, but also the whole human race" (*Essays,* p. 94). Third, "the evolutionary history of Man's search for truth" has already reached "a very high stage" (*Essays,* p. 219). "The new creatures that Paul mentioned" have already appeared outside the church (*Essays,* pp. 82, 91). Communists, atheists, and believers of other religions, by their own moral ability and truth, could ultimately enter "the community of mankind in God's will" (*Essays,* p. 213, (Ding's "Theory of Man," to be discussed in the next section). But all these proofs are essentially opposed to biblical teaching.

Ding's Cosmic Christ is not the Jesus Christ revealed in the Bible. Although he tries very hard to pull the two together, readers who respect the Bible cannot find any similarity between the two. The three basic points of Ding's theory of the Cosmic Christ "historical reformation" as the motivation for his theological deliberations; the theories provided by de Chardin; and Ding's utilitarian purpose to accommodate Christianity to Chinese Marxism) are all outside of biblical revelation. Therefore, a conflict between the two is inevitable.

Ding notices the importance of using the Bible to prove the nature of universal salvation by the Universal Christ. However, every scripture he uses refutes the existence of a Christ of universal salvation. In his articles "The Universal Christ" and "How to View Truth, Goodness, and Beauty Outside of Christianity," Ding quotes such biblical passages as John 1:1-4, 9, 14; Philippians 2:6-11; Colossians 1:15-20; Hebrews 1:2, 3; and Romans 5:15, 17. These passages do indeed reveal the pre-existence of Jesus Christ as the Son of the eternal God, his divine and human natures, his identity as the mediator in the reconciliation between Man and God (1 Timothy 2:5), and his transcendent position as the Creator, Redeemer, Judge, and Glorious Lord. However, these passages do not contain any information indicating that Jesus is a Christ of universal salvation. After all, a Christ of universal salvation does not require Man to establish a relationship with him by faith because he does not need to execute the redemption defined in the Bible. Yet, Jesus of Nazareth calls for Man's faith by his redemptive love: "whoever believes in him has eternal life," "whoever believes in him shall not perish but have eternal life," "whoever believes in him is not condemned, but whoever does not believe stands condemned already because he has not believed in the name of God's one and only Son," "whoever believes in the Son has eternal life, but whoever rejects the Son will not see life, for God's wrath remains on him" (John 3:14, 16, 18, 36). Saving faith is vital.

The truth of the Scriptures may disappoint all who want to create contradictions in the Bible. Ding is in a similar situation. From his quotation of the Gospel of John, the reader may sense the difficulty he encountered. In order to find a basis for his unbelief, Ding wished to win God over to his side by saying, "God is so generous that, although many do not acknowledge his existence and are not grateful to him, he does not care... God is unlike us, who only know how to engage in the debate about belief and unbelief" (*Essays*, p. 205).

Yet, the God of the Bible happens to be a God who cares a great deal about the difference between belief and unbelief. The Gospel of John cited by Ding is precisely a book focused on the difference between belief and unbelief. Aside from the above-mentioned passages (John 3:14, 16, 18, 36) that treat belief and unbelief as the axis (*focus* and *axis* are terms used by Ding), we notice that John used the term *believe* 98 times. His main purpose in writing his gospel was so "you may believe that Jesus is the Christ, the Son of God, and that by believing you may have life in his name" (John 20: 31). In fact it is Ding, who despite his claims, dares not allow the Bible to speak for itself. He takes certain words and phrases often out of context, but these do not help him. When he quotes John 1:1-4, 9, 14 as proof of universal salvation by the Universal Christ, you discover that what these passages reveal are the divine and human natures of Jesus Christ, who is the object and foundation of Man's faith.

Romans 5:15, 17 are two other verses that Ding has quoted on numerous occasions and in which he received much comfort. He said, "As we understand this passage of the Bible, we will feel liberated and encouraged," (*Essays*, p. 95) because God's grace "was not granted to only a relatively few believers" (*Essays*, p. 95).

However, those who utter such words cannot hide from the truth of the apostle who emphasized justification by faith.

> That is really no gospel at all. Evidently some people are throwing you into confusion and are trying to pervert the Gospel of Christ... As we have already said, so now I say again: If anybody is preaching to you a gospel other than what you accepted, let him be eternally condemned! (Galatians 1:7, 9)

Ding cannot avoid this solemn rebuke because he has indeed changed the Gospel of Christ.

The entire Book of Romans is saturated with the theme of God's righteousness and Man's justification by faith. Romans 5:15, 17 confirm and describe this theme: The goodness of God's grace absolutely and unlimitedly transcends the evil of Man's sin. God has provided salvation to human beings, but they must receive God's grace by faith—this is the unchangeable principle for man to establish a living relationship with God. Those who are saved are "justified by faith," and "have peace with God through our Lord Jesus Christ," "through whom we have gained access by faith into this grace in which we now stand" (Romans 5:1, 2). Here, Paul has not only revealed the nature of the gospel, but also intended to tell the world: "It is the power of God for the salvation of everyone who believes... For in the gospel a righteousness from God is revealed, a righteousness that is by faith..., just as it is written: 'The righteous will live by faith'" (Romans 1:16, 17). When quoting the two verses from Romans, Ding did not place them in context. He only allows them to bring comfort and encouragement to the adherents of universalism. Yet all these passage clearly teach that salvation is not universally automatic but only by faith in Christ's finished work at Calvary.

The utter difference between Ding's Cosmic Christ and the Jesus Christ in the Bible is also shown in Ding's mixing up of creation with redemption, and his replacing redemption by creation. Ding's creation is basically no different from de Chardin's universal evolution, except Ding carefully avoided the term *evolution*. De Chardin's Christ is the "internal driving force" of the evolution of the universe. Ding's Christ is the creative force or "potential force" underlying the "universal principle" of love (*Essays*, p. 113).

Concerning God's creation, the Bible has clear and unmistakable teaching: "In the beginning God created the heavens and the earth." (Genesis 1:1); "Thus the heavens and the earth were completed in all their vast array. By the seventh day God had finished the work he had been doing.... He rested from all the work of creating that he had done" (Genesis 2:1-3).

Yet, Ding speculates that "creation is not yet completed" (*Essays*, p. 278). "There is no limit to God's creation; its process is long lasting. Christ has participated and is participating in the creation of all things" (*Essays*, p. 93).

Ding said, "De Chardin would not agree with the view that God used only six days to create and then rest forever. This view is incompatible with de Chardin" (*Essays*, p. 199). He also said, "As you can tell, I relish de Chardin's theological viewpoint" (*Essays*, p. 205).

Because the term "creation" has a special meaning in Ding's theological deliberation, certain related but distinct concepts have been mixed up by him. The Bible tells us that God creates. He also takes care of, redeems and renews his creation. Hebrews 1:2-4 is very clear about these aspects: "Through whom he made the universe" refers to creation, "sustaining all things by his powerful word" refers to taking care of, and "he had provided purification for sins" refers to redemption. God's care and redemption are related to creation but should not be considered as the same. Yet in the explanation of creation, Ding prefers to view "the generality rather than details" (*Essays*, p. 199). He considers all are "creations:" "creation being a process of redemption," (*Essays*, p. 199), and "creation encompasses redemption, whereas redemption completes creation" (*Essays*, p. 278). He overemphasizes creation in order to deny redemption through Christ.

Ding also talks about redemption, but his redemption is merely "a link in the process of creation," (*Essays*, p. 93) and "a part of continuous creation" (*Essays*, p. 110). So long as it is not the genuine redemption through the blood of Christ of the Bible, Ding appears to allow some work of redemption by his Cosmic Christ on the half-finished product which is mankind. But this redemption must not contradict creation as he sees it. It must "guide the progress of the whole creation and realize the goal of unity in God," and must "be linked to mankind's efforts towards progress, liberation, democracy, and

universal love" (*Essays*, p. 96). While loudly promoting "the unification of creation and redemption," so as not to "polarize" "creation"
and "redemption" (*Essays*, p. 276). Ding allows his concept of creation to swallow up redemption completely in order to smuggle in
his concept of universalism.

Ding's publications are filled with this kind of contradiction. Yet,
behind such contradictions, he skillfully denies God's plan of salvation through Christ as revealed in Scripture. When proposing the
idea of the unification of creation and redemption, he does not hesi-
tate to toss aside the historical reality of Man's fall and its terrible
consequences. His unification is a fig-leaf to cover up the shame of
denying true redemption by his concept of creation.

Ding's focus is not on the Jesus of Nazareth as revealed in Scripture. If you were to ask him to really talk about God's redemption,
Ding says: "We cannot explain very well why the incarnation is necessary in God's creative process; nor how Christ and his crucifixion af-
fects our reconciliation with God" (*Essays*, p. 256). Ding's inability to
speak clearly on these vital doctrines of the Christian faith is natural
since he insists on viewing Christ's redemption only in the framework
of de Chardin's or his own continuous "creative process."
Furthermore, he cannot even "talk clearly" about the "fact of Christ's
resurrection" (*Essays*, p. 186). If both the incarnation and crucifixion
are regarded by him as unnecessary to his Cosmic Christ, then it is
hardly surprising he is unable to speak clearly about the physical resurrection!

What is resurrection? In an article entitled "The Truth About
Resurrection," Ding says:

> What I want to say is not that in China we have obtained some
> new evidence about Christ's empty tomb, but only to say that it is
> most appropriate to use the term "resurrection" to describe the ex-
> perience of China as a nation or of the Chinese Christians as a
> church. In our personal, national, and church life, we experienced a
> kind of resurrection from death. This experience enabled us to rec-
> ognize that resurrection is God's working rule of creation, redemp-
> tion, and sanctification in this world, his law to sustain and rule over
> the entire universe. (*Essays*, p. 8)

In another article, Ding continued:

> Although people are unclear about the facts concerning

Christ's resurrection, there are one billion people who believe that the truth represented by resurrection is very profound. This belief goes counter to common sense but has not been erased after 2,000 years. Although no one can explain it clearly, it cannot be discarded totally. Using a familiar phrase, the teaching of resurrection has its foundation among the masses. (*Essays*, p. 186)

These two articles on resurrection compel us to ask: Does Ding truly believe in Jesus Christ's resurrection? Clearly he does not. But, is it not true that his articles often mention Christ's resurrection or the resurrected Christ? Yes, but Ding's Christ is not the Christ of the Bible; the resurrection in his understanding is not that recorded in Scripture. We will discuss his basic unbelief in the biblical doctrine solely on the evidence provided by the Bible itself.

Is it true that the fact of Christ's resurrection is not well understood and that no one can explain it very clearly as Ding claims? If so, what foundation is the Christian faith that has endured 2,000 years built on? Here is the Apostle Paul's clear answer:

Christ died for our sins according to the Scriptures, that he was buried, that he was raised on the third day according to the Scriptures, and that he appeared to Peter, and then to the twelve.... And last of all he appeared to me also. And if Christ has not been raised, our preaching is useless and so is your faith. (1 Corinthians 15:3-5, 8, 14)

Paul's answer shows Ding's absurdity, for the Bible cannot be any clearer about the fact of Christ's resurrection. In the four Gospels that Ding respects, Jesus himself repeatedly foretold his death and resurrection. Every gospel describes Christ's empty tomb and his resurrection as a major event, which took place historically in time and space, according to God's plan of salvation. It became the turning point in the history of salvation and the foundation of Christian faith. Christ's resurrection is a fact not because one billion people believe in it, nor because "we experienced a certain type of resurrection from death" in our personal, national, or church life. Nor have we felt that "it was unreasonable for someone like Jesus to end in death" (*Essays*, p. 186), and thus we ought to "raise him up" out of our deep compassion (*Essays*, p. 187). Ding reduces the resurrection to a human psychological or sociological phenomenon. But the fact of Christ's resurrection is based on the historical reality that "Christ died for our sins according to the Scriptures, that he was buried, that he was raised on the third day according to the Scriptures" (1 Cor. 15:3, 4).

The reason that Ding denies the fact of Christ's resurrection is because his Cosmic Christ does not need resurrection. The idea that a universal principle that guides the endless progress of creation is in need of incarnation, crucifixion, and resurrection would be a belief that counters common sense. To Ding as to Wu Yaozong, it appears to be a belief, "I cannot accept no matter how hard I have tried" (Wu's own words on resurrection and other basic doctrines—Yaozong, p. 77). Ding has this to say about the incarnation:

> The message of the incarnation is that God himself has become a member of the human world. As to Jesus' being a male, it is incidental, much like his height and the color of his eyes. I think from a theological point of view, Emmanuel did not have to take place in a male body. (*Essays*, p. 230)

Please read the following biblical passages on Jesus birth, while considering Ding's theological thought.

"In the past God spoke to our forefathers through the prophets at many times and in various ways, but in these last days he has spoken to us by his Son..." (Hebrews 1:1-2).

"For to us a child is born, to us a son is given..." (Isaiah 9:6).

"Therefore the Lord himself will give you a sign: The virgin will be with child and will give birth to a son, and will call him Emmanuel" (Isaiah 7:14).

"You are my Son; today I have become your Father" (Psalm 2:7; Hebrews 1:5).

"I will be his father, and he will be my son" (2 Samuel 7:14; Hebrews 1:5).

These passages demonstrate that our God is a God with a plan. He did not come to this world accidentally and blindly. (It is interesting to note that the vicious cult "Eastern Lightning" which is ravaging many rural churches in China also plays fast and loose with the incarnation—in their case they claim that Christ has been re-incarnated as a Chinese woman! Some extreme feminist and New Age groups also worship God and Christ as female. So Ding's carelessness regarding the incarnation can set a dangerous precedent.)

4. The "Cosmic Christ" and Ding's Social Gospel

"In Memory of Pastor Eckerton" may be the most easily over-looked article in Ding's *Essays*. In this commemorative article of a Communist pastor, Ding expressed his inner feelings. It might serve also as an apology for some possible misunderstandings of his belief by future generations. It might also be an attempt to avoid the embarrassing fate of Pastor Li Chuwen (a Communist agent in the Chinese church in the 1950s and 1960s whose true identity was ultimately exposed during the Cultural Revolution.)[1]

This article bears great similarity to Lin Daiyu's "Flower Burial Eulogy."[2] Ding had a profound understanding of the motivation in Pastor Eckerton's decision to join the Communist Party.

> I think that Allan joined the British Communist Party as a testimony for Christ against the narrow-mindedness of the people during the Cold War, when no one truly understood Christ. Like some prophets in the Old Testament he took symbolic action to convey God's message. He proclaimed the slogan that 'truth shall overcome...' (Essays, p. 508)

Eckerton once told Ding: "The Communist Party encouraged me to be a good pastor, while my religious belief demanded that I be a good Party member" (*Essays,* p. 508).

I am not clear how Pastor Eckerton of England managed to merge Communist and Christian pastor in one person (a wisdom neither God nor man can undertake). But I know Mr. Ding's efforts in this regard have been remarkable. He can put his fundamental beliefs and the ideology of his political organization in the overall framework of Christian theological deliberation, thus merging the two systems so effectively that his fundamental beliefs have appeared to have gained a reasonable theological explanation, potentially endangering the biblical faith of the Chinese church. Yet simultaneously he wins praise and plaudits from both the deceived and his co-conspirators alike. This point becomes clear from the relationship between his Cosmic Christ and his concern for the present world system.

In his article entitled "How Should Chinese Christians View the Bible," Ding claimed that he had known a "greater Christ" (*Essays,* p. 84). However, after reading his publications about this Christ, we discovered that he has either sent Christ to a universe based on some abstract love or placed this greater Christ into a smaller framework. The former endeavor may be outside the focus of his theoretical interest, whereas the latter shows up the true nature of his faith. This smaller framework in which he wishes to limit Christ, is China's political and social reality.

Ding's theoretical interest regarding the Cosmic Christ was stimulated by the historical reforms of the Communist Party around 1949. However, when applying his theory to real life, this Cosmic Christ became the basis for uniting believers and unbelievers behind the Party and the precondition for the mutual accommodation between Three Self (that is, government controlled) Christianity, and socialism. Ding said, "The discovery of Christ's universal nature...provided a theological foundation for the all inclusive unity represented by the China Christian Council" (*Essays,* p. 32) (We note here for the unfamiliar reader that the China Christian Council and the TSPM are known as the two associations (*lianghui*) in China. This reflects the reality that both the CCC and the TSPM are both ultimately controlled by the Party through the United Front Work Department and the Religious Affairs Bureau.) This universality is manifested in the belief that Christ will also save those who do not believe in Him. If so, the vital issue of faith and unbelief is no longer a focal question in the discussion of Christian faith by Ding and his supporters.

Ding believes that the Cosmic Christ can rationally explain Communism. Here is what he says: "Is it possible to harmonize the existence of atheism with what is done by the Cosmic Christ? I think so. The existence of many things in the world can be made to be consistent with the work of Christ" (*Essays,* p. 95).

> Many contemporary ideologies and movements are no longer viewed as contradictory or damaging to God's revelation. They are a kind of help to enlighten revelation. While limited in scope, they are not necessarily hostile to the Christian faith. They may in fact be tiny lights that help us to know Christ. To view reality in this manner is certainly not to undermine the uniqueness of Christ the Son of God. On the contrary, it serves to add to his glory. (*Essays,* p. 28)

> Since we have witnessed the truthfulness, goodness, and holiness of many non-Christians who have persistently pursued the truth, we no longer think that God provides special grace only to historical Israel....

This is our understanding of the Universal Christ. (*Essays*, p. 96)

It is clear that in speaking about ideologies and movements and the many non-Christians who have persistently pursue the truth, Ding is referring to Marxist ideology, socialism, the Communist movement and revolutionary atheists. These historical events attain transformation and sublimation through Ding's Universal Christ. They will be "accepted by God in the final historical high tide," "such that.... they will have not only historical but also ultimate meaning" (*Essays*, p. 28).

Ding's mind is full of the beautiful illusions of a great crowd of Communists, humanists and revolutionary atheists. Their existence demonstrates that mankind has an enormous capacity for self-perfection. To these individuals, it is not only unnecessary to have the salvation of Jesus of Nazareth, but it is absurd to speak of it. In the words of the New Age theologian Fox, they are the "anointed ones," they "all have the nature of God," they are all the Cosmic Christ. Concerning these illusions, Ding said:

> They are atheists who do not allow themselves to engage in any crime. They are strictly self-disciplined and do not permit themselves to do anything that would harm the liberation of the people. They love mankind and are willing to sacrifice themselves for the welfare of others. They do not pursue their own good or a comfortable life. They love the people as comrades. The most important mark of revolutionaries is not hatred, but love. The true revolutionaries always have a strong sense of love. There are indeed many things in society that are hateful. But the revolutionaries hate because they love. (*Essays*, p. 141)

In these words, the readers can see the basic scheme of Ding's Universal Christ in the practical political and social scene. Ding wants to say that "without Christianity, people may also have high qualities; " (*Essays*, p. 242) without Christ's redemption, they have also attained this degree of perfection; they have revealed God in parallel with Jesus. Thus "revelation does not come from Jesus Christ alone" (*Essays*, p. 246).

This is Ding's Universal Christ. This is the entire content of Ding's Christology. The reader may ask, is this truly a common theological trend of the Chinese church during the past 40 years? Is this really a central focus of Chinese theological thought? Is this what helped the church survive under bitter persecution or caused probably the greatest church growth since Pentecost? If the answer from the overwhelming majority of Chinese Christians who are evangelicals faithful to Scripture is negative, then Ding's effort to represent Chinese Christianity and to speak for the Chinese church are both ineffective and bogus.

Notes

1. Li Chuwen was a secret Communist agent who posed as a Christian pastor. His real identity was later exposed. In 1950 he returned to China as head of the Religious Education department of the YMCA. He later became pastor of the Shanghai International Church and secretary of the TSPM. During the Cultural Revolution he was attacked by Red Guards who uncovered his Communist Party membership. He was transferred to a post in the Foreign Affairs Office of the Shanghai Municipal Government. Later he was sent to Hong Kong by the New China News Agency to become the vice-director of its Hong Kong branch.

When Li's Communist Party membership became public it astonished many Christians who were unaware of what was going on behind the scenes in Mainland China.   The former Director of the Hong Kong branch of the New China News Agency, Xu Jiatun mentions in his published memoirs that before Li Chuwen was appointed to the Foreign Affairs Office in Shanghai he was "a secret Communist Party member who undertook religious affairs work." We might add that the revelations of how the Communist Parties of the former USSR, East Germany, Romania etc. manipulated the churches in those countries and infiltrated KGB and Stasi agents at the highest levels (so that even Bishops were working for the Party) is a sober warning not to accept the highest levels of leadership of the present church in China, whether Protestant or Catholic, too much at face value. Unfortunately, many Westerners including many Christians are far too naïve in this regard.

2. Lin Dai Yu is a fictional character in a popular Chinese novel, Dream of the Red Chamber, that was written during the Qing dynasty, the last Chinese dynasty.

5

Ding's Theory of Man

Christian theology uses biblical revelation as the general principle in describing man's nature, man's relationship with God, and man's origin and final destiny. Any theory of man that betrays biblical revelations cannot be viewed as truly Christian. Of course, humanist and other theories that distort biblical revelation may constitute various theoretical systems, but they cannot provide a truthful and reasonable explanation of Man.

Ding's theory of man is humanistic and distorts biblical revelation. His theory of man, together with his view of God and Christology are the three pillars of his theological deliberation. Although in the *Essays,* Ding often skillfully hides the discussions of Man in his discussions about God and Christ, it is not difficult to see that Man is the real center of his concern. Unlike his treatment of God and Christ as abstract universal principles, he sees Man as a real, practical, and concrete entity. Ding's ultimate concern is Man, not God.

In the biblical revelation, the Christian theory of man is fully described. Man's present sinful condition resulted from the disastrous break in his relationship with God. God originally created Man in his own image, but Man fell and became a sinner because of his disobedience to God. Sin entered the world through one man, and death came from sin as the sinner's end. The sinner cannot save himself because he cannot get rid of his sinful nature. But because of God's love and his will to save Man who is dead in sin, God sent his only Son Jesus Christ to become flesh, to die on the cross in order to take away Man's sin and to propitiate God's wrath, thereby fully upholding both His love and His righteousness. Anyone who is willing to accept this resurrected Jesus as Savior may be reconciled with God and become a new creature. This new Man has eternal life, and is created in

God's image in righteousness and true holiness.

However, Ding's theory of man is different. For the sake of Man, he first speculates about a God not revealed in the Bible (see the section above.) He then discusses Man in the context of his relationship with this theoretical God. In such discussions, God's image has a broad background (the so-called entire universe) and is poetic (the lover in the universe, etc.), but in reality is abstract, empty, and weak. In comparison, Man in his evolution moves steadily from the status of a semi-finished product to a finished product or towards perfection, and thus appears to be more real, more noble, and more in a central position of the universe than God Himself.

The Bible has a strong message that without God's revelation man cannot know God nor himself. Based on this truth, John Calvin pointed out:

> It is evident that man never attains to a true self-knowledge until he previously contemplated the face of God, and come down after such contemplation to look into himself. For (such is our innate pride) we always seem to ourselves just, and upright, and wise, and holy, until we are convinced, by clear evidence, of our injustice, vileness, folly, and impurity. Convinced, however, we are not, if we look to ourselves only, and not to the Lord also—He being the only standard by the application of which this conviction can be produced. (Calvin 1993, 38)

Regrettably, Ding creates his own arbitrary measuring stick. As a result, his theological deliberation becomes an arbitrary discussion about man.

First, Ding's evasive words on mankind's sinful nature cannot hide his real intention of denying the true biblical doctrine. Ding's *Essays* generally include two kinds of language, evasive and concrete, which are difficult to distinguish. The former quotes Scripture out of proper context or cites one or two seemingly orthodox views, whereas the latter is used to express forcefully his real belief. (One can glean particular positions he holds by a careful reading of his writings as certain phrases and ideas keep re-occurring.) Thus the reader may find in the *Essays* several evasive statements about sin, such as "Chinese Christians believe deeply the need to maintain the consciousness of sin" (*Essays*, p. 85), Chinese Christians "acknowledge Man's sinfulness and limitations," (*Essays*, p. 25) and "Man is not only a sinner, but also a victim of sin" (*Essays,* p. 133).

Nonetheless, the overall message of the entire *Essays* is a thorough denial of Man's sinful nature. How do we know? From the following three points:

(1) Ding denies the absolute necessity of Christ's salvation and does not recognize His uniqueness. (But the Bible teaches that "salvation is found in no one else," Acts 4:12.)

(2) He denies salvation by faith and justification by faith.

(3) He denies the universality and reality of sin.

Regarding the first point, I need only to add the following. If Man had no sin, then Christ's redemption is completely unnecessary. Such a reason Ding understands, for he says, "Without this, salvation would not be necessary" (*Essays,* p. 316). Thus, he starts out by denying the absolute necessity of redemption, and then denies in reality Man's sinful nature. However, the Bible does not leave any room for argument. The Lord Jesus said, he came to "call sinners" (Matthew 9:13) and "to give his life as a ransom for many" (Mark 10:45). Paul said also, "[Christ] gave himself for our sins to rescue us from the present evil age, according to the will of our God and Father..." (Galatians 1:4).

Regarding the second point, we need only to add to what I have previously published on the relationship between faith and sin (see Appendix One). The *Essays* are filled with Ding's criticisms of "those [i.e. evangelicals and all orthodox Christians] who write far too much about belief and unbelief," which shows his own deep concern about this issue. His concern is motivated by a desire to erase the issue of faith from Christianity. However, the Bible emphasizes that faith is intimately related to Christ's redemptive sacrifice.

According to the Bible, the issue of belief and unbelief existed from the beginning of human history. The reason that Adam and Eve sinned and fell is because they chose "not to believe" God when tempted by the devil. Unbelief led to Man's disobedience to God and to his fall and separation from God. Therefore, Christ's salvation is intended to fundamentally solve the problem of Man's unbelief and to provide salvation to Man by grace through faith. On Christ's side, the sin offering has been made once for all on the altar. "By one sacrifice he has made perfect forever those who are being made holy" (Hebrews 10:14). "Those who are being made holy" are "those who believe and are saved" (Hebrews 10:39). On man's side, "without faith it is impossible to please God" (Hebrews 11:6). If the issue of "unbelief" remains unresolved, then the issue of "sin" can never be resolved (see John 9:35-41). Therefore, the denial of the biblical truths of salvation by faith and justification by faith cannot but involve the denial of sin and its seriousness.

Regarding the third point, the Bible has many teachings about sin's universality, reality, as well as its terrible consequences. Please note the following Scriptures:

"Jews and Gentiles alike are all under sin. As it is written: 'There is no one righteous, not even one! There is no one who understands, no one who seeks God. All have turned away, they have together become worthless. There is no one who does good, not even one....' For all have sinned and fall short of the glory of God" (Romans 3:9-12, 23).

"Therefore, just as sin entered the world through one man, and death through sin, and in this way death came to all men, because all sinned" (Romans 5:12).

"For the wages of sin is death, but the gift of God is eternal life in Christ Jesus our Lord" (Romans 6:23).

These scriptures are very familiar to us Christians who treasure the Bible, knowing that they are God's revelation and our only basis for understanding human nature. Yet, Ding, who often claims to speak on behalf of Chinese Christians, appears to deny this basic doctrine. As a result, he severely criticizes those Christians who "have universalized sin" (*Essays*, pp. 28, 114). Ding's denial of the universal nature of sin originates from his denial of the historical truth of Man's sin and fall. He is against the use of "mankind's fall and lack of goodness as the basis to proclaim sin and Christ the savior" (*Essays*, p. 91). In his view, sin is not a universal and true condition of human nature. When speaking of the manifestation of sin, he attributes the existence of some "ugly and violent" phenomena in the world to Man's "being still in the process of creation" and "far from perfection" (*Essays*, p. 96), not because of Man's being universally and truly sinful.

Ding considers himself "a Chinese intellectual cultivated in the Confucian tradition and not entirely Christianized" (*Essays*, p. 135). He is sympathetic to the ancient Confucian philosopher Mencius' teaching of the "good nature of Man" (*Essays*, Preface). Ding believes that it is impossible for Christians to uphold totally the biblical truth concerning Man within the restrictions of Chinese traditional humanism. He emphasizes:

> Having understood this background of the Chinese intellectuals, it is easy to understand why Chinese Christians are unwilling to go further in acknowledging Man's sinfulness and limitations, and to understand why they ignored God's image in Man or the movement of the Holy Spirit in the world, and why they do not easily accept the formula of total depravity. (*Essays*, p. 25)

Ding seems to be saying that God's image in Man has never been seriously damaged by sin, and that God has never said, "My Spirit will not contend with man forever, for he is mortal..." (Genesis 6:3). Therefore, his rejection of the orthodox doctrine of "total depravity" (or "formula" as he calls it) is totally reasonable.

Ding's distortion of the doctrine of total depravity is astonishing. In many of his articles he repeatedly quotes a sentence he attributes to Calvin that "Man is a five-foot tall worm." In *The Institutes*, Calvin used the term "worm" to describe Man's smallness in comparison to the universe, not in a derogatory sense (p. 53). We should like to ask Ding where else Calvin had said that Man is a worm? The Bible itself, however, has said, "I am a worm and not a man" (Psalm 22:6) and "O Worm Jacob" (Isaiah 41:14).) However, Ding misrepresents this one statement as if it represented the entire content of the Calvinistic theory of man, and as if the doctrine of total depravity could be summarized by this one sentence and thus be denied.

Anyone who is acquainted with Reformed theology knows that the term "total depravity" does not denote that Man is totally evil, nor is completely depraved in all his actions, nor has committed all kinds of possible sins, thus totally losing his conscience and desire for goodness. This is just not true. Total depravity means that sin has affected every part of Man's nature and that sin's destructive power has corrupted Man's mind, conscience, and will (see 2 Corinthians 4:4; 1 Timothy 4:2; Ephesians 2:1, 4:18). Man's sinful nature prevents him or her from doing good deeds that please God. Ding uses the concept that "Man has God's image" as an excuse to deny the doctrine of total depravity, when in fact, he is opposed to the biblical foundation of this doctrine. The Bible tells us that Jesus Christ did not redeem Man because "Man has God's image" but that he died on the cross for us because we are all lost sinners.

In his theological deliberations, Ding distorts or waters down certain truths in order to achieve his goal of ultimate denial, using a method of dilution. Sin becomes merely an "awareness of sin" that a Christian should have, or merely a "sinful inclination" (*Essays*, pp. 85-86). Please note that, sin here is no longer regarded as affecting the whole of human nature, but becomes only an awareness and an inclination. What is Ding's awareness of sin? He says,

> The awareness of sin is an awareness that not all things are very good; it should mutate into an awareness of concern, concern about the suffering in the world. Only by starting from this point can one speak of improvement and achieving a greater height (*Essays*, p. 265).

As to sinful inclination, it "merely shows that people constantly need God's forgiveness, correction, healing, and spiritual support" (*Essays*, p. 86). He means that it would be inappropriate to exaggerate the degree of Man's fall, and to consider sin as Man's totally depraved nature. He thinks that since Man has always been in the process of being created, it is quite commendable that he has kept a kind of awareness of sin about evil things during this process. To him it is sufficient for Man with such an awareness to depend on himself to sublimate, improve and elevate himself. If so, this is sheer Pelagianism—the heresy that mankind can save himself without relying on the grace of God. Of course, Ding allows that people can also accept God's forgiveness, correction, healing, and spiritual support. However, Ding appears hesitant to accept the plain message of the Bible that everyone must accept Jesus Christ's salvation by faith, repent of their sins, and to be reconciled with God.

The denial of man's sinful nature has opened up the way for Ding's man-centered theory of Man. If Ding proposes his theory of the Cosmic Christ for the purpose of selling his the theory of universal salvation, then, his ultimate goal in discussing the humanistic theory of man is to promote the theory of self-salvation. Regardless of what he has said, conceptually or metaphysically, about God, Christ, the Cosmic Christ, the essential attribute of the universe, or universal salvation, etc., his ultimate goal is to lead you to focus on Man.

(When speaking of Man, Ding becomes very excited: Man is such a wonderful piece of work! His rationality is so noble! How limitless is his power! How dignified and outstanding is his appearance and manner! In his actions, how much he resembles the angels! How much he is like gods in understanding. The cream of the universe! The spiritual chief of all things! He repeatedly recites these descriptions by William Shakespeare, totally ignoring the contradiction between these Renaissance descriptions and his own theory of man as a semi-finished product.)

Regarding the doctrine of man, we feel it unnecessary to quote excessively Ding's praises for Communists and revolutionary atheists, for they contain too much political emotion and class sentiment, which may hinder the reader from seeing the objectivity which should characterize a theologian.

Let us take a look at his concern about Mary, for on this point we may see another important ingredient of his anthropology which is humanism under a theological veneer. To express this thought, Ding carefully chooses Mary, Jesus' mother, as a starting point for theoretical discussion.

According to the Bible's objective descriptions, Mary is indeed worthy to be called a great mother. Her greatness does not lie in such Roman Catholic statements as "she was conceived with no original sin and was sinless," "she participated in redemption," or "she cooperated with Christ and played a role of mediator in God's grace" (Rahner, 181-182). Mary's greatness lies in the fact that she was an obedient "maid servant of the Lord" (Luke 1:38). No one on earth felt more directly the pain of Christ's suffering in his death, like "a sword piercing through [her] own soul" (Luke 2:35). The Roman Catholic teachings about Mary have no biblical basis. To deify Mary is as absurd as to dishonor her. Ding's praise for Mary basically developed from the Roman Catholic doctrine. After undergoing some changes by him, this doctrine becomes an important building-block for his humanistic theory of Man.

Ding's man-centered theory of man is fully expressed in the two articles entitled "Living Life One Should Have a Mission" and "From Creation to Nativity." Ding could not write much on Christ's death and resurrection to meet the theoretical need of constructing his theory of Man. However, he definitely has something to say about the incarnation, because he discovered that this "major event with universal meaning" could not have occurred without mankind's "cooperation." "Ding says:

> In the development of the God-Man relationship, the angel's visit to Mary was a sign: During the entire process of God's creation, redemption, and sanctification of the world, appeared an important minority of people, whom God expected would work with him self-consciously. If this expectation of God was not to be in vain, but to be responded to positively, then the incarnation would meet Man's conditions and receive Man's cooperation, rendering waiting unnecessary.

> The question is whether mankind was going to provide cooperation and coordination on this important matter to bring it to realization, or to be passive or even resistant, thereby delaying the progress of God's creation... When Mary was pondering the news brought by the angel, not only were God and the angel waiting for her free choice, but also the entire universe, the entire nature, the entire world were holding their breath, nervously waiting for her agreement, because the whole creation was waiting for deliverance from bondage into the glorious liberty of the Children of God. Whether such an expectation could be realized depended on Mary's response at that time. (*Essays*, pp. 182-83)

The same statement also appeared in "From Creation to Nativity," where Ding added that the incarnation was "the process by which God created that perfect world in his mind" (*Essays*, p. 254). God's purpose is to create "a harmonious world, including the present and future generations" (*Essays*, p. 254). (Ding called this harmonious world the new heaven and new earth.)

> In that harmonious world, I think that green and red traffic lights will still be needed. Traffic police will still exist, but war, murder, arrest, detention, and execution will cease to exist. However that world will not be "without differences." Differences will exist and will be much more in number than today. In this manner, life and ideology will be richer and more colorful. Otherwise, life and ideology would be too monotonous. (Essays, p. 254)

(In this passage, we cannot distinguish humor from theological ignorance or from fantasies of a Communist utopia.)

Ding then said that God "in order to attain this goal...through a long period of revelation, discipline, education, and inspiration," caused "a group of people on earth to make preparations for the incarnation (*Essays*, p. 255).

> In Mary, we saw the zenith and crystallization of that preparatory process. In Mary, God could finally expect the appearance of sufficient devotion in being willing to be the carrier of the incarnation. God and the entire universe could be said to have held their breath in anticipation of her response. Her response was relevant to all people. She had every freedom and right to say no.... However, she magnified the Lord, having been brought up this way.... She was happy to be able to participate in this creative process. In other words, she had her own view of values and correctly used her freedom in offering her cooperation for the incarnation.... It is this personal view of values instilled in a person during a long growing-up process that determines what she or he chooses at critical junctures... In the process of incarnation, Mary's agreement played a decisive role. (*Essays*, p. 254-257)

Those who honor the Bible may be shocked by these statements! Ding appears to re-write the Scriptures as he pleases. This God, who has love as his highest attribute and whose wisdom, power, righteousness, and glory are merely secondary attributes, has been restricted by Man for the first time in the history of the God-man relationship! Even his plan of redemption required Man's agreement before it could be implemented. Seeing God's supposedly has to hold his breath in anticipation of a response, mankind must have felt for the first time their own nobility, dignity and glory!

However, this sovereign God does not allow Man to develop history in such a way. According to the Bible, more than 700 years before the incarnation, God had already said through the prophet Isaiah: "Therefore the Lord himself will give you a sign: The virgin will be with a child, and will call him Emmanuel." He also said, "For to us a child is born, to us a son is given, and the government will be on his shoulders.... The zeal of the Lord Almighty will accomplish this" (Isaiah 7:14, 9:6-7). The gospel of Luke (and of Matthew) recorded the fulfillment of this prophecy. The Bible's descriptions of Mary and this event are far different from Ding's imagination.

> God sent the angel Gabriel to Nazareth, a town in Galilee, to a virgin pledged to be married...[whose] name was Mary. The angel went to her and said, "Greetings, you who are highly favored! The Lord is with you. [The] angel [also] said to her, 'Do not be afraid,

Mary, you have found favor with God. You will be with child and give birth to a son, and you are to give him the name Jesus'…. The Holy Spirit will come upon you, and the power of the Most High will overshadow you. So the holy one to be born will be called the Son of God" (see Luke 1:26-35).

After the angel revealed to her God's plan of salvation, Mary said: "I am the Lord's servant. May it be to me as you have said" (Luke 1:38).

Here, Mary did not exercise her view of values instilled in her while growing up or her freedom. Instead, she exercised her faith in God's promises—"Blessed is she who has believed that what the Lord has said to her will be accomplished" (Luke 1:45). Because of her faith, Mary demonstrated enormous obedience toward God's will. (Regrettably, both faith and obedience are things that Ding appears to downgrade. On numerous occasions, Ding mentioned that obedience is merely the sheep's response to the shepherd. It "is not the highest moral standard that mankind can achieve" (*Essays,* pp. 71, 101, 281). If Ding insists on finding in Mary the elements by which mankind can rival God, he is greatly mistaken.

Such mistakes occur frequently. Sometimes, whenever Ding quotes a Bible verse, he immediately expresses an anti-biblical view. In the article entitled "Womanhood, Motherhood, and the Nature of God," Ding said that in chapter one of Genesis we learned about God's creation of Man according to his own image—"male and female he created them" (Genesis 1:27). Then he said from another angle: "Therefore, God has not only a male, but also a female image" (*Essays,* p. 231). The Bible has clearly honored God as the standard of all creation and said that God created man and woman in his own image. But in Ding's theological deliberation, Man has become the standard of all creation. Ding views problems from the point of view that Man created God. Consequently, "God has a male as well as a female image" (*Essays,* p. 231).

Once Ding's train of thought is understood, it is not difficult to understand why his writings are always permeated with subjective humanism. Ding's starting point is always *we*—*we* are willing; *we* like; and *we* want. In other words, *we* decide what to keep or discard. *We* only want the God that *we* like. *We* mold God into a shape *we* like. In reviewing Ding's view of God and his Christology, we soon discover how much these theories are tinted by self-centered humanism.

Concerning Ding's theory of Man, it is not difficult to see that not only was he motivated by liberation theology, de Chardin's theology, and process theology, but also influenced by New Age theology's view of human nature (See "Analysis of Ding's Christology," Chapter Four of this book). In his theological deliberations, Ding makes subjective and egotistic deductions. When wanting to express his own views, he subtly quotes the ideas of others; when "introducing" these others, the viewpoints are clearly his own.

For example, when introducing the viewpoints of liberation theology, he said:

> Gospel preaching not only brings Christ to the poor, but also discovers the Christ already in the poor. Gospel preaching not only "brings Christ to" the world, but also discovers Christ among the world, because a trace of Christ is already in every person in the world. To uncover Christ in them is also gospel preaching. (*Essays* p. 192)

In these words Ding's own views on human nature are clearly brought out. In his view, there is no qualitative difference between a sinner and God. The only difference is that the Christ in Man is a little less than the Christ in God. However, little bits of an arc may ultimately form a perfect circle which is Christ or the Cosmic Christ. Ding himself often uses this analogy: "If Christ is a perfect circle, then each of us is either a long or short arc" (*Essays,* pp. 53, 96, 115). He reminds people that if you uncover the "Christ" in you "bit by bit, " then you will be able to realize self-salvation "bit by bit" (*Essays,* pp. 53, 96, 115). Ding provides a description of the process of mankind's self-salvation:

> God anticipates and works toward the appearance of a new mankind. Out of their free will, these people cooperate with God in creating truth, goodness, and beauty, as well as all kinds of valuable things... leading mankind out of a kingdom of necessity to a kingdom of liberty. (*Essays,* p. 112)

Another idea in Ding's theory of Man worthy of discussion is his idea that mankind are semi-finished products. Having appeared repeatedly in *Essays,* this humanistic idea is evidently quite satisfactory to him. However, this idea cannot withstand the light of truth. Its absurdity lies in the fact that it belittles God and cannot authentically describe Man's nature.

It does not recognize redemption, and it denies creation. It attempts to explain the phenomenon of evil in real life, while denying the objective reality of Man's fall. It denies the perfection of God's creation, and also erases the results of sin.

Let us see how Ding explains this idea of semi-finished products:

> Romans 8 tells us that "the whole creation has been groaning as in the pains of childbirth right up to the present time" (vs. 22). This is to say that the creation is not yet completed. The world and the people therein are semi-finished products at different stages in God's creative process... Our mission as semi-finished products is to be God's assistants in his creative work. While helping God, we help ourselves, to change from semi-finished to finished products. (*Essays,* p. 278)

> Man is a semi-finished product of past creation or evolution, an object of future reformation, and a force for further humanization.... Although we are only semi-finished products, God already wanted us to push history forward, advance evolution, and to promote creation. And this is exactly the process by which semi-finished products become finished ones. (*Essays,* p. 202)

Using Romans 8 as the basis for introducing his "semi-finished product" is self-defeating. What this passage proves is exactly what Ding wishes to deny. Romans 8:19-23 says:

> The creation waits in eager expectation for the sons of God to be revealed. For the creation was subjected to frustration, not by its own choice, but by the will of the one who subjected it, in hope that the creation itself will be liberated from its bondage to decay and brought into the glorious freedom of the children of God. We know that the whole creation has been groaning as in the pains of childbirth right up to the present time. Not only so, but we ourselves, who have the first-fruits of the Spirit, groan inwardly as we wait eagerly for our adoption as sons, the redemption of our bodies.

In this passage, where does it say the world and the people therein are all...semi-finished products? Clearly it talks about Man's sin and Fall, the damage of the relationships between man and God, among mankind, and between mankind and nature. In God's plan of redemption, all creation "groans" and is in "pain," (Paul's personified descriptions) expecting to be liberated from its bondage to decay. When the sons of God (those who received the sonship of God through their faith in Jesus the Savior) are manifested, all creation will also enter into "the glorious freedom of God's children."

This passage clearly gives a message about the tragic consequence of the Fall, and about God's intended salvation. Why does he re-write the passage in such a way that "the act of creation is not completed; the world and the people therein are semi-finished products at different stages in God's creative process" (*Essays*, p. 278)? Moreover, how is it that in this kind of bondage to decay and groaning and pains, the world and we become God's assistants in his creative work and at the same time...we help ourselves to change from semi-finished to finished products?

It would be easier to understand this vague concept of semi-finished products, if we simply remove the protective veneer of God and change *creation* to *evolution* in Ding's discussions. "Man is a semi-finished product of the creation or evolution of the past;" because Man is in the process of creation, he cannot help but be a "semi-finished product." In such a process, man is the subject as well as the object. "He is the object of further reformation (object), also the force behind further humanization (subject)" (*Essays*, p. 202). Therefore, Man can "promote history, promote evolution, and promote creation." If we realize that in Ding's vocabulary, *creation* is synonymous with *evolution*, then it becomes clear what he meant when he said that "God's creation has no end; it is a process of long duration" (*Essays*, p. 93), that "the world and we are in the process of reformation, in the process of God's creation, in which we are evolving from semi-finished products into better products" (*Essays*, p. 104), that "the zenith of his creation would be the appearance of a new Man in the universe" (*Essays*, p. 101), and that we supposedly await the "final completion of a human community in God's will" (*Essays*, p. 213).

What Ding means to say is that Man is the master of his own destiny. He must, and can, engage in self-perfection in the process of evolution. "Love seeks the highest good for us. All good things will ultimately not be lost. They will be perfected and elevated, until the coming state which is based on love." God is merely a kind of state whose principle is love. Man can achieve this state by himself. Ding says: "This is what we mean when we say that God is the master" (*Essays*, p. 57).

In addition, we may discover that in his theories of God, Christ and Man, Ding has a consistent concern for the present. He says:

We need to have a clearer understanding of human nature in order to create a social system that can best eliminate the self-centeredness of individuals. This social system would allow human nature to undergo a better growth. (*Essays*, p. 30)

Only by establishing a healthier social system, by practicing more reasonable distribution of wealth, with resulting prosperity, peace, joy, and advancement, can we help people see that the Christian view of the almighty Father and God is reasonable. Only then people can find a reason to thank this God. (*Essays*, p. 5)

Ding believes that the degree of perfection of the social system determines that of human nature. Only through a perfect social system can one find a reasonable explanation for Man's need of God. Socialism and Communism are the two most perfect social systems he can see. Therefore, all issues compatible to these systems, he not only "supports politically," but also has entirely "thought through theologically" (*Essays*, p. 319).

6

Conclusion

Through our discussions of Ding's view of God, Christology and theory of Man, it is clear that his theological thinking is essentially opposed to the Bible. This situation compels us to assert with regret that the *Essays* are not really the milestone of Chinese theology as claimed by Ding's supporters. They are rather evidence of his basic unbelief in the biblical gospel.

The God of history has His perfect will in placing this phenomenon before the Chinese church. We are even willing to accept this "gift" with a thankful heart. The Lord placed 450 prophets of Baal before Elijah and the Israelites so that they would not "waver between two opinions," but know that "the Lord is God, the Lord is God!" (1 Kings 18:20-39). In the history of the Christian church, God has allowed the existence of various heresies and errors. He permits both the good seed and the weeds to "grow together until the harvest" (Matthew 13:24-43). While waiting for the final harvest, God's spirit of wisdom has taught and trained many Christian disciples who can discern truth from falsehood.

We do not need to discuss Ding's "theory of the Spirit" in a separate chapter. From Ding's concept of the Holy Spirit "leading" the atheistic "Chinese revolutionaries" "to enter into deeper truth," (*Essays*, p. 143) the believer may know that *his* Holy Spirit is different from the Spirit of revelation in the Bible. Neither does Ding discuss ecclesiology according to what is taught in the Bible. His ecclesiology is "a theory of the church-state relationship," a theory of "how can hair grow without the skin[1]," "the theory of Three-Self sovereignty," or the theory of "using scaffolding[2] to manage the erection of a building." The more this kind of ecclesiology is "perfected," the less the Chinese church will be like the true church of God.

In an article entitled "A Renewed Understanding of the Three-Self," Ding strangely portrayed the Three-Self and the China Christian Council as "the scaffolding," giving an impression that he and his companions "coordinated closely with one another" only for the building of this scaffolding (*Essays*, p. 323). As to who will use this scaffolding to build, and what it is they will build, the answers given in Ding's *Essays* are rather disappointing to those who are concerned for the Chinese church.

In fact, since the establishment of the Three Self Patriotic Movement (and its twin, the subsequent China Christian Council), they have merely been the "hair" on the "skin" of the controlling political authority. As the hair, there is no reason why they should not adapt to the skin. Therefore, by calling themselves scaffolding, and by using the slogan "to build a unified spiritual and secular theological thinking in order to ensure the harmony between the church and socialism" (*Essays*, p. 376) it cannot but be a self-conscious expression of their subservience to the State. Concerning the church-state relationship, Ding said correctly "We should be on our guard if the political rulers were to claim to be pious, or to uplift the cross, or to make many promises to religion" (*Essays*, p. 67). For the same reason, we should also be on our guard if certain religious persons favored by the Communist government should proactively lead religion to "adapt" to certain ideologies, and thereby dilute or even eliminate our fundamental beliefs.

Ding said, "Theology is the church thinking" (*Essays*, p. 240). Indeed, biblical theology is the outcome of the church's Spirit-led thinking. However, not every theology is true. Those anti-biblical, anti-God and atheistic theologies destroy the very foundation of Christian faith. They, and the heresy of modernism are not the church thinking, but rather the thinking of the devil. Satan is quite capable of theological thinking (See Genesis 3:1-5, Matthew 4:3-9). So are false prophets and wolves in sheep's clothing.

This kind of theological deliberation is more dangerous than secularism as it does not confront the church openly from without, but corrupts it from within.

It will lead men to "become more and more ungodly" (2 Timothy 2:16). "Their teaching will spread like gangrene. Among them are Hymenaeus and Philetus who have wandered away from the truth... and destroy the faith of some" (2 Tim 2:17-18). It is to be feared that there are a number of leaders and theologians in modern Chinese official church circles who are in danger of leading many astray.

"Nevertheless, God's solid foundation stands firm, sealed with this inscription: 'The Lord knows those who are his' and 'everyone who confesses the name of the Lord must turn away from wickedness'" (2 Timothy 2:19). These words of Paul are still relevant today for the Chinese church.

Notes

1. Editor's Note: This Chinese expression—*pi zhi bu cun, mao jiang yan fu*—is a Chinese patriotic saying. The original full text can be translated as: "If there is no skin, where will the hairs be?" This saying is interpreted to mean: "If there is no China, where will the Chinese be? They will become slaves of other powerful countries." Ding uses this expression to encourage the Chinese Christians to join the Three-Self Patriotic Movement, which is the full name of Three Self. However, Ding has always placed greater emphasis on the "patriotic" element than on the "Three Self" elements (i. e. the church should be self-governing, self-supporting and self-propagating).

2. Editor's Note: *Jiao shou jia* is a term used in China today to refer to scaffolding for building.

Appendix One

An Analysis of Recent Works by Ding Guangxun

Li Xinyuan

I

Recently, Bishop Ding Guangxun—who is recognized as "the principal spokesperson for contemporary Chinese Christianity"—published several articles, saying that he wanted to "discuss some issues that others dared not talk about." These articles are:

1) "Discussion of a Profound Question among Christians," on page 285 of the Ding Guangxun *Essays*, published in 1998 by Yilin Publishing Company (hereafter referred to as "Issues");

2) "A Call for Adjustment of Religious Ideas," published in the September 4, 1998 issue of *Renmin Zhengxie Bao* [*Report of the Chinese People's Political Consultative Committee*] (hereafter referred to as "A Call");

3) "Old Theological Thinking in Need of Adjustment and Renewal," published in the March 5, 1999 issue of *Renmin Zhengxie Bao* (hereafter referred to as "Renewal").

In these articles, Ding earnestly sought to respond to the call by Chairman Jiang Zemin of the Chinese Communist Party (CCP) to "guide mutual accommodation between religion and socialist society." He earnestly sought to "water down" and "to not talk about," and even to "purge" "all religious things that are incompatible with socialism" (see "Renewal" and "A Call"). He sought to guide people to "value political guidance for theological thinking," etc.

Those who know Ding are not surprised by these views because his theology has always contained a lively political element and a keen political sense. On numerous occasions, he taught his students that "politics cannot be separated from theological discussions; some-times, theology is refined politics" (*Essays,* Introduction). However, in these articles, faithful Christians cannot help but notice his attitude toward the Christian faith behind his fervent political emotion. He seems to have changed his enigmatic position of many years and no longer hides his deep hatred of the fundamental truths of the Christian faith such as salvation by faith, justification by faith, Christ's Second Coming, the Day of Judgment etc. He began to directly proclaim to the church and to the world his unbelief, as the standard bearer for the "Faction of Unbelief."

This article will not comment much on Ding's political position on "accommodation"[1] of Christianity to certain ideology, or on certain "adaptation" undertaken by the Three-Self Movement of which Ding is the principal spokesperson. This is not surprising. History shows that the Three Self, first represented by Wu Yaozong and then by Ding, has been in this process of adaptation for the past half century. Because of this adaptation, there was the longest, most widespread, and most profound persecution on Chinese soil against Christians who could not adapt. Because of this adaptation it was possible for the government to realize their desire to ideologically water down Christian belief.

As a complex politico-religious figure and a product of a peculiar political environment, Ding and the TSPM may continue to engage in their adaptation work. However, I would urge Ding not to water down Christian beliefs or to ignore or even purge the gospel truth. Yet Ding cannot help, as he has often said, but to keep diluting and purging. Therefore we must, for the sake of our faith, strengthen our beliefs and stress the gospel truths in which we believe.

II

In "Renewal," Ding gave an example of what he means by watering down and avoiding basic gospel truth. He said: "There are many passages in the Bible about how God cares, protects, and blesses all of mankind, including both those who believe in Christ and those who do not. This is *normal* religious faith."

But what is *abnormal* religious faith? (It is of vital importance to note that in China only those who adhere to "normal" religious beliefs approved by the TSPM and the government can expect toleration; those whose faith is labeled as *abnormal* can expect persecution.) Ding goes on:

> However, there are people in the church who consider themselves to have the orthodox in their faith. They emphasize the contradiction and antagonism between those who believe and those who do not. They say that only the believers will be saved and go to heaven after death whereas the unbelievers will not be saved and will go to hell after death. Based on this view, they earnestly evangelize, trying to persuade others to believe, thus rendering Christianity a religion of antagonism between believers and unbelievers, a situation which is incompatible with socialism.

This statement has two meanings: denial of the biblical truth of salvation by faith and vilification of believers who insist on this truth, and desire to evangelize unbelievers.

Let us look at some biblical teachings that Ding has often avoided:

"Just as Moses lifted up the snake in the desert, so the Son of Man must be lifted up, that everyone who believes in him may have eternal life. For God so loved the world that he gave his one and only Son, that whoever believes in him shall not perish but have eternal life. For God did not send his Son into the world to condemn the world, but to save the world through him. Whoever believes in him is not condemned, but whoever does not believe stands condemned already because he has not believed in the name of God's one and only Son" (John 3:14-18).

"Jesus answered, "I am the way and the truth and the life. No one comes to the Father except through me" (John 14:6).

"Salvation is found in no one else, for there is no other name under heaven given to men by whom we must be saved" (Acts 14:12).

"I am not ashamed of the gospel, because it is the power of God for the salvation of everyone who believes....For in the gospel a righteousness from God is revealed, a righteousness that is by faith from first to last, just as it is written, "The righteous will live by faith." (Romans 1:16-17).

"But the Scripture declares that the whole world is a prisoner of sin, so that what was promised, being given through faith in Jesus Christ, might be given to those who believe" (Galatians 3:22).

"And, once made perfect, he became the source of eternal salvation for all who obey him" (Hebrews 5:9).

(Other passages include John 1:12-13, 8:24, 20:31, 11:25-26; Acts 2:21, 16:30-31; Romans 5:21, 10:9-11; Ephesians 2:8-10; Colossians 1:13-14; 1 Thessalonians 5:9; and 1 Timothy 2:4-6.)

To those who believe in God's Word, the meaning of the above passages is very crystal clear. They will not tolerate any deviation from the vital truth of salvation by God's grace only through faith in the atoning blood of Jesus Christ as held by the church for nearly 2,000 years.

Ding, as bishop and principal spokesperson, often quotes the Bible in his speeches and articles. He must have realized that the above-quoted passages express the fundamental characteristics of the Christian faith. May I ask him: If you know these passages mean that believers can be saved and unbelievers cannot, why do you criticize those who uphold this fundamental truth and accuse them of "considering themselves to have the orthodox faith," and of wrongly "emphasizing ...antagonism" and of "being incompatible with socialism"?

Ding is offended by those who "based on this, earnestly evangelize and try to persuade others to believe." Yet he should understand that the gospel does not mean that the believers sit idly by and watch unbelievers go to hell. The gospel is summarized in the passage "For God so loved the world that he gave his one and only Son, that whoever believes in him shall not perish but have eternal life" (John 3:16). This verse shows the perfect will of God, "who wants all men to be saved and to come to a knowledge of the truth" (1 Timothy 2:4) and "not wanting anyone to perish, but everyone to come to repentance" (2 Peter 3:9). This gospel so despised by Ding contains the Christian's duty to fulfil the Lord's commission as stated by Paul: "Woe to me if I do not preach the gospel!" (1 Corinthians 9:16). Ding is free not to preach the gospel. But he should not condemn those who do so.

All who understand the Christian faith know that to earnestly preach the gospel of salvation through Christ alone is not stressing the antagonism between believers and unbelievers, but actually eliminating this antagonism. For the glorious gospel "destroyed the barrier, the dividing wall of hostility, by abolishing in his flesh....His purpose was to create in himself one new man out of the two, thus making peace, and in this one body to reconcile both of them to God through the cross, by which he put to death their hostility"

(Ephesians 2:14-16). It is out of a great love that believers share this Gospel of reconciliation with nonbelievers. This love is ultimate, surpassing ideological, class, and political boundaries.

Ding has a bad habit of finding political harm out of the most innocent elements of the Gospel. Over 40 years ago Wang Mingdao criticized him for this fault. At that time, Ding, according to Wang, "avoided discussing the differences in belief and accused those who were determined not to cooperate with 'the unbelievers' for maintaining the purity of faith." He accused them of being "divisive" (Mingdao 1996). Today, following the same line of reasoning, Ding tries to link the question of belief and unbelief with the "destruction of the great unity of the Chinese people" (Mingdao 1996). He thus deliberately politicizes a fundamental truth of the Christian faith—that faith in Christ is of vital importance in deciding the eternal destiny of every human being.

III

Ding also tries hard to dilute the basic principle of the Christian faith—justification by faith. In his writings he raises the following "problem:"

> Some people wrote to me, expressing their uneasiness and lack of peace about the belief that it is God's righteous will that believers would go to heaven after death while nonbelievers go to hell, regardless of their moral condition; furthermore, they feared to discuss this question openly.

He thus wants to bring it out into the open for discussion. Ding claims:

> …"righteousness" was originally an ethical and moral concept. However, the hypocritical scribes and Pharisees of Judaism derived many rules which ordinary people could not comply with in order to oppress them and convince them of their unrighteousness. Jesus was opposed to them. Paul being loyal to Jesus proposed the concept of justification by faith in the New Testament books of Romans and Galatians in order to free people from such bondage, and let humanity be liberated.

Here we see Ding's subtle attack on the key doctrine of justification by faith.

Catholicism of Medieval Europe repressed people also. To resist its system of repression, Martin Luther, like Paul, once again raised up the banner of justification by faith....Therefore, historically speaking, religious pioneers like Paul and Martin Luther proposed justification by faith as a means to extend justice, to oppose the dark powers of religious authority, to purify religion, to simplify religion, and to obtain freedom for the people. Thus it is clear that justification by faith has a progressive meaning. It is a banner of liberation, the purpose of which is by no means to send people to hell.

After such watering down, we can no longer see any similarity between Ding's justification by faith and that taught by the Apostle Paul and Martin Luther.

Paul said in Romans 1:16-17:

Because it [the gospel] is the power of God for the salvation of everyone who believes: first for the Jews, then for the Gentiles. For in the gospel a righteousness from God is revealed, a righteousness that is by faith from first to last, just as it is written: The righteous will live by faith.

In Romans 3:22–27:

This righteousness from God comes through faith in Jesus Christ to all who believe. There is no difference, for all have sinned and fall short of the glory of God, and are justified freely by his grace through the redemption that came by Christ Jesus. God presented him as a sacrifice of atonement, through faith in his blood. He did this to demonstrate his justice, because in his forbearance he had left the sins committed beforehand unpunished—he did it to demonstrate his justice at the present time, so as to be just and the one who justifies those who have faith in Jesus. Where, then, is boasting? It is excluded. On what principle? On observing the law? No, but on that of faith.

(Chapters 3 through 8 basically talk about justification by faith.)

In Galatians 3:11, 12, 14, and 22, clearly no one is justified before God by the law, because, "The righteous will live by faith." The law is not based on faith; on the contrary, "The man who does these things will live by them." He redeemed us in order that the blessing given to Abraham might come to the Gentiles through Christ Jesus, so that by faith we might receive the promise of the Spirit." "So the law was put in charge to lead us to Christ that we might be justified by faith."

The above Scriptures are typical of Paul's teaching about justification by faith. They clearly and unmistakably state that "all have sinned and fall short of the glory of God." The righteousness of man (whether it be the righteousness of legalism or the righteousness of those who are morally upright, according to Ding) can never meet the standard of salvation set up by God's perfect justice. God, because of his grace and love, opened a living way so that by believing in Jesus Christ people may be redeemed and justified freely (see Romans 3:24).

Paul's objective in preaching justification by faith is absolutely not to send people to hell. Rather, he hoped that everyone who is already dead in sin might live through faith in Jesus Christ.

> Because of his great love for us, God, who is rich in mercy, even when we were dead in transgressions, made us alive with Christ. For it is by grace we have been saved, through faith—and this not from ourselves…, it is the gift of God…Not by works so that no one can boast. (Ephesians 2:1-10)

However, Ding does not believe in these basic gospel principles. He only believes that the progressive meaning of justification by faith is merely a banner of liberation to allow human nature to be liberated. In his attempt to water down the truth of justification by faith, Ding's humanism is very obvious. If he could see God's humanitarian spirit in the commandment of Sabbath keeping, why couldn't he see Jesus, Paul and the Bible similarly? When he examines God, Christ and Christ's work of salvation, God's Word, human nature as truly revealed in the Bible, and other doctrines, such as justification by faith in similar manner, we cannot expect him to utter words respectful of the Bible and in accordance with biblical truth. He can only see a God who would not throw people into hell because of their lack of faith and a Jesus Christ who needed not to bleed and die on the cross.

Let us read a further passage of his:

> In our country today, more and more Christians find it difficult to accept the viewpoint that focuses on faith rather than deeds. For example, a pastor wrote to me: "My conscience would not allow me to preach the message that unbelievers would go to hell after death." The reason is simple. He saw many who have not accepted

the gospel of Christ, such as Zhang Side, Lei Feng, and Jiao Yulu,[2]
yet have demonstrated a character of self-sacrifice for others. How
can we harden our hearts to say that they are now in hell?

These are moving words, filled with his characteristic cleverness
in which he always skillfully uses other people's examples to express
his own views. However, they are also a terrible distortion of biblical
truth.

To simplify the Christian gospel to nonbelievers as being only
that "those who do not believe will go to hell after death" may be
"unpleasant" and "frightening," though biblically true. But Ding does
not just want to discuss whether the preaching method is too simplis-
tic. His true intention is to deny the truth and centrality of justification by faith. If it were simply a question of preaching style, that
could certainly be changed. For example, evangelicals do generally
preach positively from such texts as "God so loved the world that he
sent his only begotten son so that all who believe in him shall not
perish but have eternal life" (John 3:16). However, preaching in this
way would probably not be acceptable to Ding. For the fact that all
who believe in him shall not perish but have eternal life also implies
that all who do not believe in him will not receive salvation and will
perish. This is unacceptable to Ding's universalism.

Ding's basic intention is to show that an upright man according
to moral standards or the yardstick of a political organization will not
go to hell even if he does not accept the gospel of Christ. Where,
then, will he end up? Jesus Christ did not mention any destination
other than eternal life and eternal death. If that nonbeliever is not in
eternal death (hell), he must be in "eternal life" (heaven). But we
want to know, how did he receive eternal life without believing in
Jesus? Jesus said, "I am the way and the truth and the life. No one
comes to the Father except through me" (John 14:6). But this central
truth has been abolished by Ding.

Peter said, "Salvation is found in no one else, for there is no
other name under heaven given to men by which we must be saved"
(Acts 4:12). This truth has also been abolished by Ding.

Paul said, "I do not set aside the grace of God, for if righteous-
ness could be gained through the law, Christ died for nothing!"
(Galatians 2:21). Sadly, Ding appears happy to set aside the grace of
God. Does he really dare claim that Christ died on the cross for

nothing? Yet this is the thrust of his arguments.

I may add that Ding's view of the Bible is also ultimately controlled by political considerations. In *Issues,* Ding quotes a long biblical passage from Matthew (25:31-46) and says, it is a very important passage, which is certainly true. However, from his conclusions, we discover that he has either not understood this passage or has intentionally distorted it because of political considerations. Any faithful reader of the Bible would not misinterpret this passage, but Ding's interpretation is shocking:

> Thus at the last judgement, God will not question whether you have believed or not, but what your attitude is toward the poor and helpless. In other words, God is concerned about morality and ethics. Our God is so generous and loving; he will not throw people into hell just because they do not believe in him. (*Essays*, p. 288)

Even more amazing are his thoughts based on this passage:

> In the past 40 years, countless people in our country have diligently engaged in the great effort of rescuing the poor and helpless, trying to help them to cast off poverty, achieve prosperity, and then acquire wealth. Isn't this in accordance with this biblical passage? (*Essays*, p. 288)

When quoting this Bible passage Ding seems to be under an illusion. Are these the words of Jesus, or Marx? Are they a revelation of the situation in the kingdom of heaven, or a description of the present world? What is it exactly?

Those who do not wish to distort this passage and are willing to understand it can consult relevant passages as Matthew 24:23, Matthew 7:21-23, and John 13-17 (particularly the command "you shall love one another" that the Lord Jesus gave to his disciples before he departed this world and returned to the Father). These passages show:

1. Matthew 25:31-46 are Jesus' words of caution to his disciples when he was prophesying about "His coming and the end of the world." The Lord cautioned them to watch and wait as faithful and wise servants, just as he did when he said to them in the Sermon on the Mount, "not everyone who says to me, 'Lord, Lord,' will enter the kingdom of heaven" (Matt. 7: 21, 22). Only those who have obeyed the will of the Heavenly Father and lived out his command to love

one another could enter.

2. This passage contains nothing that suggests Ding's specula-tion that those who do not believe can enter the kingdom of heaven by deeds alone. What the Lord Jesus wanted to do is to distinguish between those who have faith with action from those who have faith without action (not true believers) among those who say to him, "Lord, Lord."

Our Lord never contradicts himself. If he were a God who does not care whether you believe or not, then all the teachings in the Bible would have to be rewritten.

IV

We have noticed that in "Renewal" and "A Call," Ding quoted a statement of Marx and Engels: "Following every major histori-cal change of the social system... people's religious ideas will un-dergo changes also." He said excitedly that this statement had lent "considerable theoretical support" to his "watering down," "refusing to speak," and even "purging" the "unadaptable" factors in the Chris-tian faith.

Nobody should interfere with Ding's use of the Marxist materi-alist historical view to guide his own thinking. However, we cannot sit idly by and watch him trying to change the Christian faith in order to force the Chinese church to adapt to atheistic ideology. The reason is very simple. The Bible states:

"Jesus Christ is the same yesterday and today and forever" (He-brews 13:8).

"They will perish, but you remain; they will all wear out like a garment. Like clothing you will change them and they will be discarded. But you remain the same, and your years will never end (Psalm 102:26-27).

"I the Lord do not change" (Malachi 3:6).

"Your word, O Lord, is eternal; it stands firm in the heavens" (Psalm 119:89).

"Heaven and earth will pass away, but my words will never pass away" (Matthew 24:35).

"Every good and perfect gift is from above, coming down from the Father of the heavenly lights, who does not change like shifting shadows" (James 1:17).

Since the God we believe in is a God who never changes, the Jesus Christ in whom we believe is a Lord who is the same yesterday and today and forever, and God's words on which our faith is based are the source of truths that can never be abolished, is it not a strange thing that, according to Ding, our faith can be changed beyond recognition following major historical changes in the social system?

When the prophet Daniel was taken captive to Babylon, he experienced and faced a great historical change. The Jews were a tiny minority in a hostile society. Yet, his faith did not change as a result. This prophet of God trusted God through thick and thin. He was even willing to be thrown into the lion's den to remain loyal to God. He was uncompromising in his faith. It was precisely his unyielding spirit and his powerful testimony that caused the Persian King Darius to say: "I issue a decree that in every part of my kingdom people must fear and reverence the God of Daniel. For he is the living God and he endures forever" (Daniel 6:26-27).

Yet the behavior of the Israelites who were called God's chosen people was just the opposite. God, in his grace and mercy, led them out of bondage in Egypt, but they would "soon prostitute themselves to the foreign gods of the land they are entering. They will forsake me and break the covenant I made with them." What was the outcome of the Israelites' "change of religious ideas"? God said: "On that day I will become angry with them and forsake them; I will hide my face from them, and on that day they will ask, 'Have not these disasters come upon us because our God is not with us?'" (Deuteronomy 31:16-17)

However, such historical lessons may not be able to weaken Ding's resolve to change the faith. In his preparation for the change, we cannot but notice one of his purges. What is he purging? "A Call" gives another example:

> In Christianity there are people who are enthusiastic about the arrival of the end of the world....On the surface, this kind of religious view does not have anything to do with patriotism. But in reality, if the end of the world is near, what use is there for us to speak about patriotism, socialism, Three-Self patriotism, the construction of the motherland..., etc.? How can theologians who hold this reli-

gious view have any emotional concern for the well being of our nation?

Ding claims that there are certain things in religion which are incompatible with socialism. Some must be discarded immediately, others gradually. It appears that by singling out the idea that the end of the world is near, Ding considers it among the items that must be discarded immediately.

But eschatology and the prophecies of Jesus' coming again are not the exaggerations of some people in Christianity, but biblical revelation which takes up a considerable percentage of the sacred text:

> Jesus answered: "Watch out that no one deceives you. For many will come in my name, claiming, 'I am the Christ,' and will deceive many. You will hear of wars and rumors of wars, but see to it that you are not alarmed. Such things must happen, but the end is still to come. Nation will rise against nation, and kingdom against kingdom. There will be famines and earthquakes in various places. All these are the beginning of birth pains." (Matthew 24:3-8)

> For then there will be great distress, unequaled from the beginning of the world until now—and never to be equaled again. If those days had not been cut short, no one would survive, but for the sake of the elect those days will be shortened (Matthew 24:21-22).

> At that time if anyone says to you, "Look, here is the Christ!" or, "There he is!" do not believe it. For false christs and false prophets will appear and perform great signs and miracles to deceive even the elect —if that were possible. See, I have told you ahead of time. "

> Immediately after the distress of those days "the sun will be darkened, and the moon will not give its light; the stars will fall from the sky, and the heavenly bodies will be shaken."

> At that time the sign of the Son of Man will appear in the sky, and all the nations of the earth will mourn. They will see the Son of Man coming on the clouds of the sky, with power and great glory. And he will send his angels with a loud trumpet call, and they will gather his elect from the four winds, from one end of the heavens to the other. (Matthew 24:23-31)

Since Peter had personally heard the Lord Jesus' teaching regarding the end of the world, he said, "The end of all things is near. Therefore be clear-minded and self-controlled so that you can pray" (1 Peter 4:7). Peter said:

First of all, you must understand that in the last days scoffers will come, scoffing and following their own evil desires. They will say, "Where is this 'coming' he promised? Ever since our fathers died, everything goes on as it has since the beginning of creation." But they deliberately forget that long ago by God's word the heavens existed and the earth was formed out of water and by water. By these waters also the world of that time was deluged and destroyed. By the same word the present heavens and earth are reserved for fire, being kept for the Day of Judgment and destruction of ungodly men. But do not forget this one thing, dear friends: With the Lord a day is like a thousand years, and a thousand years are like a day. The Lord is not slow in keeping his promise, as some understand slowness. He is patient with you, not wanting anyone to perish, but everyone to come to repentance. But the day of the Lord will come like a thief. The heavens will disappear with a roar; the elements will be destroyed by fire, and the earth and everything in it will be laid bare. Since everything will be destroyed in this way, what kind of people ought you to be? You ought to live holy and godly lives as you look forward to the day of God and speed its coming. (2 Peter 3:3-12)

The apostle John also said:

Dear children, this is the last hour; and as you have heard that the antichrist is coming, even now many antichrists have come. This is how we know it is the last hour. They went out from us, but they did not really belong to us. (1 John 2:18-19)

Jesus' coming again and the last days are conclusively described in Revelation, the last book of the Bible. In his old age, after experiencing numerous trials, John wrote by the inspiration of the Holy Spirit about the One "who is, and who was, and who is to come, the Almighty" (Revelation 1:8). He also described the judgment before the great white throne, and the new heaven and new earth (the coming down of the new Jerusalem). Jesus himself finally confirms these truths: "He who testifies to these things says, 'Yes, I am coming soon'" (Revelation 22:20). Upon hearing the promise "I am coming soon," John expressed his hope, comfort, and joy in the following words: "Amen. Come, Lord Jesus."

Since the entire Bible concludes with the Lord's promise "I am coming soon" and the disciple's response "Come, Lord Jesus," how is it Ding can accuse some in Christianity of exaggerating the very backward theological viewpoint of the coming of the end of the world?

Very clearly, there is a conflict between biblical eschatology and

Ding's own concerns with social and political issues. This conflict once again reveals Ding's complexity. On the surface, Ding appears to be serving two masters. But in reality his primary loyalty always remains with Caesar. He always masks his true beliefs so that many have been deceived. They blindly follow him in engaging in certain theological construction (e.g. church construction or construction of Chinese theology). This only helps Dings to become more effective in his agenda of further undermining the gospel. Many Chinese Christians whose eyes have been opened now openly accuse him of undertaking theological destruction rather than construction. His attempts to water down justification by faith and to discard the Second Coming are only part of his destructive agenda, which he and his supporters have admitted, is a long-term campaign to remove the entire Chinese church from its evangelical moorings.

V

In addition to the above-mentioned articles published in various newspapers, Ding published recently his *Essays*. The publication of this collection was hailed as "a major milestone in the history of Chinese theology" (See *Tianfeng*, 1999, Vol. 1). This accolade may be an overstatement. But in a certain sense it is appropriate; it is a milestone that may lead Chinese Christianity along the destructive path of liberalism and unbelief.

These *Essays* reveal the complex thinking of their author. The *Essays* are a mixture of Ding's own humanistic view of life with Communist characteristics, his historical materialistic method of thinking (i.e. Marxist), his utilitarian principle of using theology to serve political ends, process and liberation theologies, the theological views of Teilhard de Chardin[3] and the views associated with the New Age Movement. None of these can really be considered as "theological thought with Chinese characteristics" (*Tianfeng*, 1999, Vol. 1).

The only Chinese characteristic of Ding's collection is the tight integration and synchronization of his theological thinking with contemporary Chinese political culture. The *Essays* do not provide any appropriate theological conclusions regarding the lives and spiritual testimonies of Chinese Christians during the past half century under the reality of repressive rule of false ideology and power politics. The precious lessons of their sufferings and the glories of their spiritual triumphs—so desperately needed by China and the West today—are completely ignored. In building a Chinese Christian theology faithful to biblical revelation, Ding has been more destructive than constructive.

Members of Chinese "official Christian circles" and Ding's admirers have used many nice words to describe him (see *Tianfeng* and *Essays,* Foreword). However, like the false prophets denounced by Ezekiel (see Ezekiel 13:1-16). Ding has sought to whitewash over his fundamental denials of biblical revelation. Chinese Christians should keep a clear head on this point.

Notes

1. The Chinese term *shi ying* could be translated as either "adaptation" or "accommodation." In the context of the history of the persecuted church in China, accommodation has been used more frequently. This translation, however, will use either word to represent the meaning of *shi ying,* depending on the context of the passage in question.

2. These are individuals who, since the founding of the People's Republic, have been promoted by the Communist authorities as models of good citizenship, soldiery, and officialdom, respectively.

3. De Chardin (1881-1955) was a Catholic theologian and biologist who went to China in 1929 and participated in various research efforts surrounding the "Peking Man." He supported the theory of evolution and was rebuked by the Roman Catholic Church for his views. In 1948, he became a member of the French Academy of Sciences. His works include *The Beginning of Man, The Future of Man,* and *Man in the Universe.* He established in Beijing a biological research institute and published a magazine on biology. He was a promoter of the theory of "creation-evolution."

Appendix Two

Three Articles by Ding

A. Discussion of a Profound Question among Christians

Ding Guang Xun's Speech delivered at an ecumenical conference in northeastern China, 1996. Also in *Essays*, Yilin Publishing Company, 1998, Nanjing, pp. 285-289.

As a bishop and the chairman and president, respectively, of the two national Christian associations (Chinese Christian Three-Self Patriotic Movement and China Christian Council), I have often received letters from church officials throughout the country. Some of them expressed anxiety and lack of peace about the belief that, regardless of one's morality, believers will go to heaven after death while non-believers will go to hell. The adherents of this view assert that this is due to God's "righteousness." Yet, these officials were afraid to discuss the issue with others.

I am willing to discuss it openly.

"Righteousness" was originally an ethical and moral concept. Since childhood we know that we ought to act righteously in the world. However, the hypocritical scribes and Pharisees of Judaism (Jesus on many occasion rebuked them for their hypocrisy), defined "righteousness" by rules with which people could not comply in order to oppress them and convince them of their unrighteousness. For example, to keep Sabbath on the seventh day was originally a commandment with a humanitarian spirit. It allowed people to rest and to remember God one day every week. However, the Pharisaic party (*dang*)[1] formulated many strict regulations to limit people. On the Sabbath, all secular activities must cease and there were even regulations on the distance one might travel (one faction said that one might only travel a stone-throw's distance). Harvest was prohibited, and sheep that fell into wells could not be rescued. According to historical records, these kinds of regulations numbered in the thousands. Those who obeyed these regulations were considered righteous. Otherwise, they were regarded as disobedient to the commandments of God. Jesus was opposed to the Pharisees saying, "they tie up heavy loads and put them on men's shoulders," and "they do not practice what they preach." Paul was loyal to Jesus. He declared justification by faith in the New Testament books of Romans and Galatians in order to liberate people from such bondage, thereby allowing mankind to receive liberation. Through the principle of justification by faith, Paul released people from the inhumane rituals and ceremonies related to circumcision, the Sabbath, etc., that had been set up by the Pharisees, thus enabling the Christian gospel to break through the framework of Judaism and to spread to the Gentiles. As a result, Christianity emerged from being a small sect of Judaism and evolved into a major world religion.

Catholicism of the European Middle Ages also bound people in this manner. At that time, European Catholicism forcibly placed strict ecclesiastical rules upon the people, and promoted the system of indulgences. Under this, if someone in a believer's household died, the church would encourage the family to purchase indulgences from the church for the dead, so that his or her stay in purgatory would be shortened according to how much the family purchased on his or her behalf. To resist this repression, Martin Luther, after Paul, once again raised up the banner of justification by faith. The [Lutheran] church he founded has continued to this day. In Chinese it is called the "Justification by Faith Church" (xin yi hui).[2]

Thus, historically speaking, Paul and Martin Luther were progressive religious pioneers who proposed justification by faith as a means to extend justice, to oppose the dark power of religious authority, to purify and simplify religion, and to pursue freedom for the people. From this example one can see that justification by faith is defined by progress. It is a banner of liberation—not to send people to hell.

In the 19th and 20th centuries, many foreign missionaries came to our country. Many of them were anxious to recruit Chinese to become believers, thus linking "justification by faith" with "heaven and hell" in their teachings. Many people in our country accepted these teachings, because of their eagerness to go to heaven. This resulted in the distortion of the original message behind justification by faith. They claimed that God does not ask what kind of life you have led— selfish, or righteous and self-sacrificing. All he cares about is whether you believe or not. If you do, regardless of how selfish and harmful you are to others, or whether you have betrayed your country and your friends, you will enter heaven to enjoy eternal bliss after death. On the other hand, if you do not believe, regardless of how much you have contributed to others and to society, you will certainly go into the eternal fire of hell. These missionaries declared that morality is useless and that God does not look at the good deeds of man with favor. As a result, they denied the ethical and moral content of the gospel, and made God a selfish and unjust God who insists that belief in himself is good, but unbelief is evil. Naturally, this is not the image of God that is described in the Bible.

[EDITORS' NOTE: This is, of course, a complete caricature of the evangelical Gospel. Christ, Paul, Luther, Calvin and Wesley all taught that justification leads to sanctification in the lives of all true believers.]

In our country today, more and more Christians find it difficult to accept this viewpoint which focuses on faith rather than deeds. For example, a pastor wrote to me: "My conscience would not allow me to preach the message that unbelievers would go to hell after death. " The reason is simple. He saw many who have not received the gospel of Christ, such as Zhang Side, Lei Feng, Jiao Yulu,[3] who were upright and showed self-sacrifice for others. How dare we to say that they are now in hell?

For such co-workers who fearlessly wrote to me to express the difficulties hidden in their hearts regarding their faith, I maintain an attitude of sympathy and understanding, not rebuke.

I believe that the God who was manifested by Christ is a loving God. Above all His other attributes is God's love. This view of God does not allow me to see him as a cruel and violent God who is willing to send thousands upon thousands of people into the eternal fire of hell. In our big cities, a single obstetric hospital welcomes many new lives into the world, giving indescribable joy to their parents. God knows well that a great majority of people will never become believers while in this world, yet he continues to create more people every moment. If what awaits them is the eternal fire of hell after several decades of living in this world, then he is not a god of love, but a fearful ruler of hell as believed by some of our country folk. Have we Christians been so influenced by this kind of belief that we imagine our God to be such a horrible deity?

The scientist Einstein pointed out that the development of a fearful religion into one of morality is a major step in the history of the evolution of religion.

The four gospels in the Bible (Matthew, Mark, Luke, and John) all talk about the life of Jesus. From these accounts, we know that although sometimes Jesus spoke of heaven and hell, please read the passage in Matthew 25:

> When the Son of Man comes in his glory, and all the angels with him, he will sit on his throne in heavenly glory. All the nations will be gathered before him, and he will separate the people one from another as a shepherd separates the sheep from the goats. He will put the sheep on his right and the goats on his left.

> Then the King will say to those on his right, "Come, you who are blessed by my Father; take your inheritance, the kingdom prepared for you since the creation of the world. For I was hungry and you gave me something to eat, I was thirsty and you gave me something to drink, I was a stranger and you invited me in. I needed clothes and you clothed me, I was sick and you looked after me, I was in prison and you came to visit me." Then the righteous will answer him, "Lord, when did we see you hungry and feed you, or thirsty and give you something to drink? When did we see you a stranger and invite you in, or needing clothes and clothe you? When did we see you sick or in prison and go to visit you?" The King will reply, "I tell you the truth, whatever you did for one or the least of these brothers of mine, you did for me."

> Then he will say to those on his left, "Depart from me, you who are cursed, into the eternal fire prepared for the devil and his angels. For I was hungry and you gave me nothing to eat, I was thirsty and you gave me nothing to drink, I was a stranger and you did not invite me in, I needed clothes and you did not clothe me." They also will answer, "Lord, when did we see you hungry or thirsty or a stranger or needing clothes or sick or in prison, and did not help you?" He will reply, "I tell you the truth, whatever you did not do for one of the least of these, you did not do for me."

It is clear from the above Scriptures that on the day of the last judgment, instead of asking whether you have believed, God will ask what attitude you have had toward those who are poor and helpless. In other words, God is really concerned about morality and ethics. Our God is so generous, so loving. He would not send people to hell for not believing in him.

This is a very important passage. Today, there are still Christians in our country who have overlooked it, quickly turning the pages. During the past 40 years, countless citizens have been diligently engaged in the great engineering effort of rescuing those who were poor and helpless, helping them to cast off poverty, achieve prosperity, and then acquire wealth and abundance. Isn't this akin to the message in this passage? We Christians should be more diligent in this area.

In the whole Bible, from the Old Testament to the New, there are many, many passages that proclaim ethics and morality. Six out of the Ten Commandments are about ethics and morality. The entire collection of Proverbs is about "persuading men to do good." Jesus said, "The Son of Man did not come to be served, but to serve, and to give his life as a ransom for many." (The "Son of Man" refers to Jesus himself.) Here, Jesus did not regard redemption as opposed to service. He said "and," not "but," meaning that he would sacrifice his life for the people and also serve them. We should not use redemption to deny service. In church pulpits and in seminary classrooms, we ought to preach with greater frequency the full gospel in accordance with the Bible.

Christianity has many teachings, including not only justification by faith, but also God being love, God's continuous creation, the incarnation, the resurrection of Christ to renew all things, the gift of wisdom by the coming of the Holy Spirit, the Sermon on the Moun etc. The greatest commandment is to love God and love others as yourself, doing to others what you would have others do to you, and not to be served but to serve. Paul said, "Now these three remain; faith, hope, and love. But the greatest of these is love." It is clear that love is greater than faith. How can we overlook this? The message of the Bible is very rich. Today, if we promote a doctrine without considering its original historical background and use it to exaggerate the contradiction between belief and unbelief, then we will destroy the unity of the people and provoke endless divisions. If so, what kind of testimony will we bear?

Uplifting morality is the strong point of Christianity and other religions. China is an ancient, civilized nation, which respects morality, reverence, and rituals. To Chinese intellectuals, particularly, preaching on ethics and morality is more attractive and appreciated than preaching about heaven and hell.

B. Old Theological Thinking in Need of Adjustment and Renewal

By Ding Guang Xun, published March 5, 1999 in *Renmin Zheng Xie Bao* (*Chinese People's Political Consultative News*).

I am a member of [official] religious circles, belonging to Christianity. Ever since Chairman Jiang Zemin's announcement many years ago "to guide to a mutual accommodation between religion and socialism," I have often pondered over this issue. I recognize that socialism is the best social system in human history. To render a mutual accommodation between Christianity and socialism is an excellent topic for discussion.

There are different levels of accommodation. Ours should not stop at the level of public expression. It should have an ideological foundation, meaning old theological thinking should be adjusted and renewed. Those faith-based items that are incompatible with socialist society should not be mentioned, or at least should be diluted. At the same time we should promote and expand things that are beneficial to socialist society. This is the adjustment to theological thinking that we are now promoting.

There are, for example, many Bible passages on how God cares, protects, and blesses the whole of mankind—both those who believe in Christ and those who do not. This is "normal" religious faith. However, there are people in the church who consider only themselves to have the orthodox faith. They emphasize the contradiction and antagonism between those who believe and those who do not. They say that believers will be saved and go to heaven after death whereas unbelievers will not be saved and will go to hell. Based on this view, they earnestly evangelize and try to convert others, causing Christianity to become a religion of antagonism between believers and unbelievers—a situation which is incompatible with socialism.

Chinese theology while in the midst of construction certainly cannot tolerate a theological view that exaggerates such contradiction and opposition that destroys the great unity of the Chinese people.

In recent months, the Chinese Christian Three-Self Patriotic Movement and the China Christian Council called on all Christians in the country, particularly theologians, to pay close attention to the question of political guidance of theological thinking. A series of national and regional conferences were held to discuss how to make some necessary adjustments in theological thinking. The response has been quite good. One of the reasons is that after these years of [political] education, [political] study and reflection, more pastors and teachers have begun to feel that they should no longer follow traditional customs in their teaching. In other words, they have begun to recognize the necessity of liberating theological thinking, and of daring to innovate.

The following comments by Marx and Engels provide us with considerable theoretical support: "Following every major historical transformation of the social system, people's views and ideas also changed, which means people's religious ideas would be changed also" (*Marx-Engels Reader*, vol. 7, p. 240). We hope that in several years time, the theological outlook of Chinese Christianity will be totally transformed, becoming better adapted to our country's socialist society, and functioning more as light and heat in international Christianity.

C. A Call for Adjustment of Religious Ideas

By Ding Guang Xun, published September 4, 1998 in *Renmin Zheng Xie Bao* (*Chinese People's Political Consultative News*)

I would like to put two important statements together for us to understand. One was spoken by Chairman Jiang Zemin: "Positively guide the mutual accommodation of religion with socialist society." The other was written by Marx and Engels: "Following every major historical transformation of the social system...people's religious views and ideas will undergo transformation also.... In other words, people's religious idea will be changed."

In China, we can hardly wait for our religious ideas to change, following the great changes that have occurred in our country's social system. We cannot be satisfied with remaining at the level of just expressing our political support [for the Communist Party]. We must see the transformation of religious ideas. We must see religion itself totally transformed.

This is how I view Chairman Jiang's statement. On the surface, it appears to be aimed at Communist cadres—to guide the mutual accommodation of religion and socialist society. But to us in religious circles, this statement should be a summons, calling us to work diligently towards the transformation of every religion so that religious ideas are compatible with socialist society. This includes the need to eradicate those things that are incompatible with socialist society. Judging from what Marx and Engels said, the changes in our religious ideas during the past half-century have been too few indeed. [EDITORS' NOTE: Ding reveals himself as a true Marxist here.]

Since the 1920s and the 1930s, Jinling [Nanjing] Seminary has been an institution of Christian higher education, relatively willing to accept new ideology. It has been considered to be "modernist." Through its publications, faculty, and graduates it has indeed provided new blood to Chinese Christianity. However, in recent years, its activities in this regard have decreased, and many backward theological ideas in the church have to a certain extent occupied the seminary. For example, there were some Christians who passionately exaggerate the arrival of the end of the world. This exaggeration has also crept into Jinling. They say that the spread of the AIDS virus is God's punishment on man and a signal of the return of Jesus and the destruction of the world. Such religious views do not appear to have anything to do with patriotism. In fact, if the end of the world is near, then what use is there for us to speak of patriotism, socialism, Three-Self patriotism, the construction of the motherland... etc.? How can theologians who hold such religious views have any concern for our nation's wellbeing?

If this is the situation at Jinling, which is known as the highest educational institution of Chinese Christianity, then one may easily imagine how little basis of support there is for the Three-Self Patriotic Movement actually has among Chinese Christians as a whole.

The point is that we must be realistic and should not over-estimate the achievements of the Three-Self Patriotic Movement and the 'patriotic' organizations of various religions. The reality is not what Marx and Engels had anticipated: the people's religious views are not so easily changed.

As for Chairman Jiang's statement, we in religious circles should treat it as a call to use the beneficial political conditions of today to bring about the transformation of religious ideas, that our transformation will not stop at the level of political speeches and expressions of support, but will be manifested through the watering down of all religious ideas that are incompatible with socialist society and the strengthening of those that are compatible. All of us in all religions can discuss which items are incompatible with socialist society and which should be discarded immediately or gradually, as well as which new concepts are compatible and thus should be promoted, with the aim of transforming the face of religion.

Notes

1. *Dang* (party or group) is the Chinese term used to describe a political party. However, the Chinese term has considerable negative connotation given its historical application to groups that were formed without official approval, and which were perceived to be interested in causing social disruption and political subversion.

2. *Xin Yi* is usually defined as "honesty." This is the Chinese name for the Lutheran Church.

3. See Note 2 in Appendix One.

Bibliography

Bush, Richard C. 1970. *Religion in Communist China*. Nashville & New York: Abingdon Press.

Calvin, John. 1993. *Institutes of the Christian Religion*. Translated by Henry Beveridge. Grand Rapids, Mich.: Eerdmans.

China & Ourselves magazine. May, 1990.

De Chardin, Pierre Tielhard. 1968. *Science and Christ*. London: Collins.

De Chardin, Pierre Teilhard. 1978. *The Heart of the Matter.* Translation of *Le Coeur de la Matiére*, "A Helen and Kurt Wolf Book." William Collins Sons & Co. Ltd. and Hartcourt, Inc.

Enns, Paul. 1989. *The Moody Handbook of Theology*. Chicago: Moody Press.

Erickson, Millard J. 1991. *Chrisitan Theology*. Grand Rapids: Baker.

Gardner, John. Interview with Bishop Ding in *China and Ourselves*. November, 1979.

Feuerbach, Ludwig Andreas. 1997. *The Essence of Christianity (1841)*. Beijing: Commerical Press.

Fox, Matthew. 1988. *The Coming of the Cosmic Christ*. San Francisco: Harper & Row.

Guangxun, Ding. 1999. *Ding Guangxun Wenji*. [*Collected Essays of Ding Guangxun*]. Nanjing: Yilin Publishers.

Guangxun, Ding. "The Progressive Nature of Revelation." *Tianfeng*, 1999.

Interview with Bishop Ding. *One World* magazine, March 1988.

Johnson, E.H. "Notes on the Church in China." Lutheran World Federation Marxism & China Study Documents No. 4. 1. 2. 10. August 1973.

Jones, Francis P. 1962. *The Church in Communist China*. New York: Friendship Press.

Leung, Ka-lun. 1996. *Wu's Understandings of Christianity and Its Relation to Chinese Communism*. Hong Kong: Alliance Bible Seminary.

Livesey, Roy. *Understanding Deception: New Age Teaching in the Church*. Oakdale, Minn.: Religion Analysis Service, Inc.

Mingdao, Wang. 1967. "Women Shi Weile Xinyang" (*We Because of Faith*), appended to *Wushi Nian Lai* (*Fifty Years*) [Wang's autobiography]. Bellman House, Hong Kong.

Mingdao, Wang. 1955. *We Are for Our Faith*. Treasuries of Wang Mingdao. Taichung: Conservative Baptist Press.

Rahner, Karl. 1969. *The Teaching of the Catholic Church*. New York: Alba House.

Spangler, David. 1980. *Conversations with John*. Elgin, Ill.: Lorian Press.

Spangler, David. 1981. *Reflections on the Christ*. Forees, Scotland: Findhom Foundation.

Tienfang. Christian Communications Ltd., Hong Kong.

Whitehead, R. L., Ed. 1989. *No Longer Strangers: Selected Writings of K. H. Ting*. New York: Orbis.

Wickerai, Philip L. 1988. *Seeking the Common Ground*. New York: Orbis.